Global Sales Channel

5X revenue in 12 months with Distributors, Resellers and Referral Partners

by Andrea Brown and Belinda Brown
globalsaleschannel.com

For my Jack and India. Every breath I take has been for you.

With appreciation of those who came before me shedding blood and tears so that this black woman could become a corporate leader.

Andrea

For my mother, who disconnected motherhood from martyrdom, changed the narrative of a generation to suit her ambition, and modeled a career I aim to emulate.

Belinda

Contents

Introduction	4
Understanding the Basics	6
Working Out if Channel Sales is Right for You	13
The Importance of Research	18
Benefits and Challenges of a Channel Sales Strategy	25
Developing a Winning Channel Strategy	31
Channel Strategy Templates	42
Marketing	59
Partner Agreement Templates - Reseller and Referral Partner	70
Supporting Internal Teams	82
Onboarding	87
Packaging your product for partners	99
Ditch the Fluff. Make Channel Measurable.	105
Realistic First Year Expectations	109
Leadership: Challenge Your Channel Teams	111
Partner Relationship Manager (PRM)	113
Make friends with Finance	116
Cross Cultural Communication	121
Partner Marketing	123
Partner Announcement Template	127
To give leads or not?	128
Partner Enablement	131
Job Description Templates	133
Becoming an Invaluable Partner	136
Glossary	139

Introduction

Like many books this one was born out of years of knowledge, experience and a dose of frustration.

We have seen organizations triple revenue in 12 months with killer channel programs as well as those that have failed miserably.

We fell in love with resellers many moons ago. They have entrepreneurialism running through their veins, the ability to be agile, move fast with a hunger to succeed. Not to mention the characters who constantly keep us entertained and on our toes with their ideas and antics!

A good channel program is a fantastic addition to or sometimes alternative to direct sales when it is understood and done properly. The pandemic has increased the number of organizations launching channel programs. We all saw what happened when we could not travel. Having local partners protects organizations from that but more importantly can fast track sales with rapid go to market opportunities and results.

Belinda and I approach sales from two different angles. An expert in market research, brand development, and marketing, Belinda has worked with some of the world's leading brands in retail, FCMG, beauty and pharmaceuticals to provide actionable insights that guide decision makers.

> *For some organizations life quite literally depends on the validity and thoroughness of the research. That is the starting point before anything else. It is the behind the scenes work that no one sees but everyone relies upon. If you get it wrong your exposure to risk is of catastrophic proportions.*
>
> *Having worked in this field for so long it is such a strange concept that companies go head first into sales and marketing plans without having done proper research and discovery. Large enterprises are still flying a guy to take a look at a few countries, have a few meetings, google a bit, present his findings and then use that as the foundation for the entire business strategy!*

Belinda Brown

Andrea's experience is in the go-to-market stages. With years of working with the world's leading print, technology and telecommunications brands she has seen first hand the joys and pitfalls of channel sales strategies.

> *I have spent much of my career watching people get it wrong in channel, myself included. Guess work gets wrapped up in the latest channel strategy. Insert corporate bingo words of your choice. I often knew things were not right but was not in a senior enough position to rock the boat so did what I was told or what would be accepted to keep the pay cheque.*
>
> *It was not until I got into more senior roles and started doing consulting that I saw the difference when you can actually steer the ship the way you want to based on what you know and have learned.*

Andrea Brown

This book is an accumulation of both unique viewpoints. 30 years experience in seeing both what works and what does not. 30 years experience of seeing companies go gungho into programs and countries without doing their due diligence and then all scratching their heads a year later when it has failed.

> *We have seen savvy channel managers drag things out for 3 or 4 years under the premise of "it takes a while to build brand awareness in a new territory" before people start to question the ROI.*

Who will benefit from this book?

- **Channel Managers** - Get ideas, strategy and a disaster recovery plan
- **Leadership Teams** - Understand how you get the best return
- **International Growth Teams** - Guidance on where, what and when

Where are you in your indirect sales channel journey?

Know nothing and are curious?

Have an underperforming existing channel?

Need to start one from scratch?

Wherever you are, this book will help you level up with guidance and practical tools.

Understanding the basics

Scaling revenue is the main challenge faced by most businesses. Many have an in-house sales team but those sales people only have a fixed number of maximum hours for each day. Hiring more salespeople to increase your revenue is one of the ways, but one that will increase your operating expenses, lower your operating income and therefore eat away at your profit margins.

Having an indirect sales channel can be a game-changing strategy which will give you all the benefits of hiring more salespeople without the usual capital operating costs. The basic premise of a channel sales model is that your channel partners become your advocates and evangelists marketing and selling your products and services on your behalf. What's in it for them? They receive financial reward by way of a commission or a discount for helping organizations to generate leads, close you business and expand existing commercial relationships.

The Difference between Channel Sales and Direct Sales

- With channel sales a business sells its products and services via a third party partner.
- With direct sales, the company sells its products and services directly to the consumer.

Companies can choose to exclusively use a direct sales model or exclusively use a channel sales model or have a hybrid sales program involving both direct and indirect channel sales.

Where channel is involved, partners are expected to generate new business and/or help support the execution or fulfillment of business in local regions. In contrast, in the case of direct sales, it is the in-house sales team that is responsible for increasing revenue. This may involve a mixture of inbound sales and outbound methods, where the prospective leads are identified, qualified and then turned into closed won business.

Channel Sales Explained

Channel sales include a middleman or a third party company who helps your company to promote, sell or distribute your products and services. You are outsourcing a function of your sales.

Channel sales strategy is about building partnerships with third parties in order to get a wider reach for your products and services to facilitate business growth. Increased exposure for your products and services that will ultimately lead to increased sales, revenue and gross profits.

Partnering like this allows you to leverage the existing customer network of an established local company. This comes at the cost of giving part of your revenue away in the form of a discount or commission.

What is important therefore is to calculate if the increase in sales volume makes up for the reduced profit margins in the long run. Note long run! Channel sales like any business function requires time to bed in and become established. In the short run setting up a channel can be expensive. Although it can happen, I would never bank on or be blinded by short term success.

Using Channel Sales to Facilitate Business Growth

Channels sales strategy is usually implemented as a part of a business growth effort. Here are the 3 ways in which channel sales can help increase business revenue:

1. Local partners own local relationships. Customers often prefer to buy from them. Someone they know or a local company they feel more confident about helping them if something goes wrong.
2. Partners can offer new go to market avenues like third-party marketplaces or a bundled solution.
3. Channel partners help you reach new geographical regions.

A channel sales program is not for every organization but is still one of the best ways to facilitate business growth. However, there can be challenges.

Understanding Channel and Direct Sales Conflict

There can be conflict with your direct sales team. This all really comes down to two things: reward and recognition.

- Who gets paid for what (reward)
- Who gets the glory (recognition)

Some would say that this is easily solved by having the direct sales team focus on one region while the indirect sales channel focuses on another. Not a bad idea but also not always practical. Later in the book we delve into Hybrid channel programs which, in most cases, are often the best way to go.

Types of Channel Partnerships

- Affiliate Partners
- Resellers
- Referral Partners
- Technology Integration Partners
- Value-Added Resellers
- Consultants
- Distributors
- Managed Service Providers
- Agents
- Dealers
- Influencers
- Marketplace
- Independent Retailers
- Global Systems Integrators
- Associations

Channel Partnership Types

Tip: Having a hybrid of partner types often works best

Choosing the right model for your business is key to channel partnership success

- Associations
- Consultant
- Global Systems Integrators
- Independent Retailers
- Marketplaces
- Agents
- Wholesalers
- Resellers
- Referral Partners and Affiliates
- Value-Added Resellers (VAR)
- Influencers
- Distributors
- Dealers

Referral Partners

Referral partners are popular sales channels for both Software as a Service (SaaS) and digital goods. The concept of a referral partner is: someone (a person or a company) identifies an opportunity and refers the lead to your business. The business then takes ownership of that lead and manages the sales cycle. Partners can be paid a small fee for submitting qualified leads and/or receive a fee if the business closes.

Referral Partner BOOST: Lead quality can make all the difference:

- Unnecessarily lengthening the sale cycle
- Your team can end up spinning their wheels on an opportunity that is all wrong and should not have got through the net in the first place

You can choose to offer referral partners an additional fee for submitting better qualified leads. This can be helpful in encouraging partners to be more invested in the partnership and progressing from chucking a lead blindly over the fence to asking additional questions first, qualifying leads in and out and saving your team time. This is where partners start to add value.

Affiliates

Affiliates may be organizations that are involved in the sales cycle and have a relationship with your prospects but do not want to be directly involved in selling on your behalf.

They will usually be happy to make a warm introduction or announce you to their membership. Here it may be a conflict of interest for them to receive a commission so that should be discussed. It is important to understand the *what's in it for them* if it is not for financial gain. It may be providing end to end resources for their members. are responsible for affiliate marketing and promoting of your product and only getting paid once the sale is made. The vendor maintains ownership and ongoing management of the customer. Referral partners are a great way to boost local brand awareness.

> *Tip: Remember how one organization defines these categories can be quite different to how another does so. Make sure you are clear with both internal and external teams about how you define them.*

Resellers

Resellers can receive a discount or commission. They often represent more than one vendor's products. They are less opportunistic and more of a business partner who will have a dedicated team and strategy to promote your product or solution.

Which one you go with often depends on the partner preference as well as local dynamics. For example in a local region where you need to have a local office to trade and be registered for local taxes etc this can be a barrier for international organizations who simply do not initially have those things in place and it can be cost prohibitive to do so at the start. A local reseller does and makes the transaction in local currency easier.

Value-Added Resellers (VAR)

Value-added resellers are different from the resellers in that they add features or services to an existing product and then resell it as an integrated product to the final users. The additional features or services added by them are above and beyond the features of the standalone product.

Value-added resellers are most often seen in the case of SaaS, electronics and the IT industry. It is common to see them bundle software applications with the hardware or bundle two software solutions that they supply together.

Distributors

Distribution channels provide products directly to the Resellers and VARs. Some distribution channels are agents, websites or businesses that serve as intermediaries between the companies that produce the product and the final buyer. Some Distributors may also allow end customers to purchase from them although this can be seen as a conflict of interests.

Wholesalers

A wholesaler is a type of distributor who usually specializes in getting the products that will later be purchased by the consumer via a reseller or retailer.

Wholesalers tend to have sales representatives who work to sell their products to the retailers. Wholesalers buy in bulk from the source company at discounted rates. They then add their profit margin and sell to the retailer.

This model originated from traditional bricks and mortar B2B typical of your local corner shop or bodega with physical products or hardware. Today this model has evolved and can also be seen online and though less common, with services.

Independent Retailers

An independent retailer is a business owner who has a retail business that is not tied to any major brand or franchise. For example, an entrepreneur who has founded and runs a clothing boutique without the support of a parent company, is known as an independent retailer.

Dealers

Dealers sell the products directly to the final consumers but work differently from the retailers who sell several variations of a wide variety of products. For example, the business owner who sells and leases cars directly to the final consumers is known as a dealer.

Agents

In this channel sales strategy, agents are those intermediaries who do not have any ownership over the products and services that they are selling. Agents are those who facilitate deals between buyers and sellers, assisting with the negotiation process.

For example, a real estate agent or broker is not the owner of the property being sold to the buyer. However, they are responsible for overseeing the process until an agreement is reached and the sale is closed.

Consultants

Consultants come in all shapes and sizes often wrongly getting put on the bottom of the value pile. They can be a one person operation often coming from the industry they now consult in. Don't underestimate consultants. They often have a very close relationship with their network and can be the most trusted (by the end client) of all partner types making them extremely influential. Consultants may be vendor agnostic - impartially recommending a solution they believe is best. As a result they may not accept a commission or any sort of fee in order to protect that position.

Marketplace Partners

Online marketplaces are used to house complimentary solutions. Good examples of this within the technology sector include solutions that integrate with each other. The marketplace may process the transactions or may just act as a referral source passing on leads to their listed partners. There may be no immediate financial gain for the owners of the market place or for every sale they may get a portion of the total amount or a referral fee. Less tangible benefits for the marketplace are positive brand associations and "stickiness". This happens when a client has so many solutions woven together affecting so many different parts of their business that it then makes it extremely difficult for the end user to move to a competitor.

Influencers

We have all heard of influencers in social media. Influencers are usually individuals that have a good following. They have built up trust with their audience and can then talk about any products and services to a captive audience who ultimately become potential consumers. Today influencers have become a critical part of indirect sales partnerships.

> *Tip: It is uncommon these days for partners to have to invest in stock keeping of hardware. So much is now driven by software, licenses and services that can be activated remotely combined with on demand ordering with fast fulfillment. This removes a barrier to entry for partners making it simpler and easier to get started.*

Working out if channel sales is right for you

In order to assess whether a channel is the right sales model for your business, you need to think about a number of key aspects in relation to the current state of your company, your product or solution, sales processes and internal resources.

Throughout the course of this book we will help you understand the factors for determining whether channel sales is the right fit for you or not.

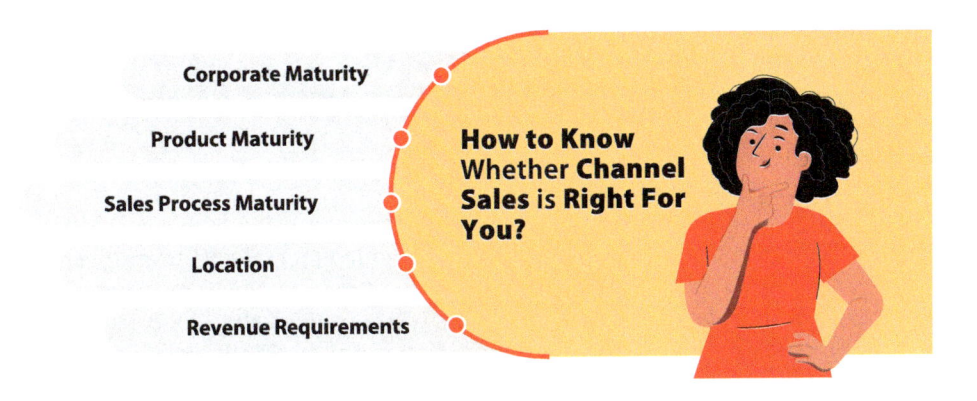

How to Know Whether Channel Sales is Right For You?

- Corporate Maturity
- Product Maturity
- Sales Process Maturity
- Location
- Revenue Requirements

Corporate Maturity

A common misconception is that this is related to the size of the organization. It is not. Small, mid sized and large enterprise organizations can all benefit from channel and can all have challenges with channel programs. The size and maturity of the business will affect which challenges they have, how they should execute and what the potential benefits are.

	PROS	CONS	DECIDING FACTOR
Small Business	Less spend on direct team and local offices	Lack of resource to police leads to partner cowboys	Start small in one or two regions where you can visit often, control, learn and grow.
Mid Sized Business	Ability to scale quickly and duplicate direct success	High risk of direct/indirect conflict	Clearly articulate your partner program internally and externally
Large Enterprise	Compliments direct sales, additional lead generation, can help establish new markets and identify where to place direct teams	Often more complex products and solutions more difficult for partners to sell	Simplify what you want partners to sell leading to greater ROI for them and higher rate of success for you

Product Maturity

To simultaneously launch a product or service and launch a partner program. That is a question that comes up a lot. While we have seen this as both a joint direct/indirect as well as exclusive channel strategy, we would not recommend it. You simply do not know enough and everything is simply too new. New product. New partner. New internal processes. You have not established enough data to benchmark and have no relationship of trust with the partner.

This is why most organizations start with a direct model. Even if it is only for a limited time, sell it yourself, be sure it is sellable and has good market fit. Then once you have established a workflow that you are confident works, even in a limited way, you can then consider channel to support your expansion. Remember you should always be teaching partners how to sell your solution. If they are 100% teaching you then they own the show. They will know this and may at some point hold you to ransom, controlling all the intellectual property and opportunities.

Sales Process Maturity

There is no need to recreate the wheel. Start with your direct sales value proposition and winning pitch deck. Channel sales should always start by looking at works really well from a direct perspective. There will be things that need rewording or making ready for an external audience. Map out the sales workflow and have documented battlecards including things like:

- The sales cycle from prospecting to closing
- Key Triggers
- Common Blockers
- Where you win
- Answer Objections

Therefore if you do not have a sales process that is mature and has all the right elements in place you are not ready to introduce a channel program.

Lengthier and more complex sales processes make it more difficult for your channel partners to sell your products and services. Shorter and simpler sales processes are ideal for channel partners. We call this productizing for partners.

With the channel you are selling twice. Once to the partner and then helping them sell to their end user. Having a clear and repeatable process is important. If you do not have one, hold off on launching a channel program until you do. An attempt to introduce channel too early can put an immense amount of stress on the business as a whole.

Location

Where your head office and regional sales teams are located affects your channel strategy. Let us imagine you have well established and successful local sales offices everywhere. There would be little need for partners. Partner programs commonly work best when they are filling a gap where you do not have a regional office or sales team. This also reduces the chance of direct and indirect sales conflict which we discussed earlier.

What you want a partner to do and how much autonomy you plan to give them is also a consideration. Let us imagine you want partners to sell but you intend to fulfill all the support and service requirements yourself. It will be important to have partners that are geographically easy and inexpensive enough for your teams to get to.

Channel programs can also be divided geographically, allocating territories to partners with added exclusivity if you wish, although we are not a big fan of that unless a partner has really earned their stripes.

Revenue Requirements

We have seen organizations launch channel programs only to do a u-turn 12 months later when they realize it takes more time and resources than they thought. Channel is not a quick win rodeo. If your corporate objective is quick revenue generation to satisfy investors or get acquired I would caution against a channel strategy. Direct sales strategies give you much tighter control on the ability to generate rapid upswings in revenue whereas channel sales is all about compound growth.

Quite often in a new market you may initially give away a lot such as free hardware accessories to help demo your product or subscription months in order to establish a few lighthouse examples of the brand. The same is true with channel partners. They need help establishing your brand in their local markets. Add to this that if you have simplified your product or solution for partners, as we suggest, they are not going to be selling your full capabilities. In practice this can mean a good number of sales in year one from partners but a relatively low profit margin as a result of things like entry level products and discounts. It is our responsibility as channel managers to ensure the partner keeps close to the customer, checking in and handling any concerns, constantly building their understanding of the customer requirements and the relationship. That way when it comes time to renew we have an end user who loves us, loves the product and is ready to expand. This is a great strategy that we have seen work well many times. Just remember that it does take time and the clock starts again with every new partner.

Let us take a look at some real examples

Step 1: #mykidscoulddoabetterjob

Storytime

> A tech company in the 90's had seen success in the U.S over 5 years of hyper growth. It seemed like a natural part of their evolution to expand internationally.
>
> They look at the massive opportunity in Germany and decide that the DACH addressable market will be their target.
>
> They send someone from finance to go to Germany to assess. They spend a week in Germany and come back confirming the opportunity. There was a spreadsheet.
>
> Two years later the entire European operation collapses after circa $3m investment.

What went wrong?

1. Germany might be big geographically but often industries are close-knit networks brought closer by online communities like LinkedIn.

Take a look at this post showing what can happen when you get it wrong. #mykidscoulddoabetterjob

What I have not shown, which is more painful, are the comments from others agreeing and the attempt by the company to offer an apology which was met with a "I've been messaging you for three months - nothing. I post on LinkedIn and you respond in 3 minutes".

The point being when it comes to channel we can afford to mess up less. Unlike direct sales this affects your reputation with both the end user and the reseller community.

If the end user hears and sees the negativity they may dismiss or not consider your product. Additionally, the reseller can also pass on their negative view of your product recommending against it to the end user who was otherwise neutral.

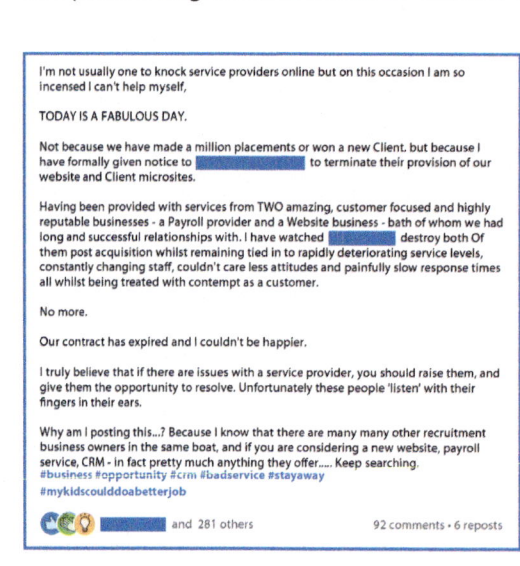

Resellers have spent years nurturing relationships and simply do not want to take the risk that one product could tarnish

that. They are risk averse. So you have a double whammy. You must take every precaution not to get it wrong. Especially in the beginning. If you are going to mess up, do it later! Once you have established a brand presence and reputation.

So back to our failed attempt to conquer Germany. They messed up and word spread. They were barely out of the gate and having to explain and answer negative connotations.

2. Sending a member of your team that fancies a trip to Europe and comes back with a few anecdotal comments heavily influenced by personal perspective is not research. "You do not understand our market" will be the first assumption/conclusion.
3. Opening in a new market was a cash drain. In place of a real plan was an enthusiastic "let's go for it" approach all based on the giddiness of the potential. Hey! Sometimes you luck out and that works, but boy if it doesn't you are in deep do, do.

What should they have done?

Start with a smaller more manageable market in an English speaking country where they could more easily communicate and support.

What was crucially missing was research.

The importance of research

If you are really unsure:

- Whether a given market is right for you
- If your product or solution will sell in a new region
- The price point you are considering will work

Doing some research with a qualified firm can provide data-driven insights to prove to yourself, decision makers and stakeholders that you are making the right decision. Quantitative and qualitative insights can inform your decisions ahead of hiring any external teams or wasting resources with partners before you are sure. What can you not afford to get wrong? Start your thinking there.

What kind of questions are you trying to answer?
Do you have the internal capabilities to design your own project?
Are you doing quantitative or qualitative research?
Does the potential market have the infrastructure to do a survey online?
Are you optimized for mobile?

Consult with a market research firm (we think GazelleGlobal.com is pretty good 😃) to outsource the entirety of your research project or to take off your hands the parts that are a stretch for your internal teams.

Selecting the right research partner for your channel project

Vetting a research partner is just as important as vetting potential channel partners. Vetting global research vendors and suppliers will ensure you are not left high and dry and right back where you started.

- First, check the firm's references. Ask the firm directly for references or talk to colleagues (or even competitors) who have used their services. If the firm is reluctant to provide references, this is a red flag. Make sure to ask not only how the work was, but what was the experience of working with the firm. Don't underestimate the importance of a good working relationship in addition to high-quality work. Check out directory listings for the firms and read through testimonials or reviews.
- Talk to other companies/colleagues in the industry that have used the vendor's market research services.
- Again, if firms are reluctant to provide these insights, it is a good indication that you may run into some issues moving forward with them. That being said, understand that a single bad review or a complaint from a competitor is not always indicative of a bad company. You have the responsibility to know what you need from a vendor or supplier and this should inform your decision as well. They should have examples of successful projects similar to yours.

Expertise in a given area

- This is key when assessing whether or not to move into a given market.
- Does your vendor or supplier have experience in this area?
- Can they provide examples of projects they have done in the region?
- Do they have partners on the ground in a given area?

All projects in a given area are not created equal. Make sure to be clear with your research partner about your demographic expectations and give them as much information up front as you can. The more info they have, the better sense you will have about their capabilities in a given potential market. Be cognizant of firms that promise you the world, literally. If everything you ask them warrants a yes, that can be a red flag. Everyone can not be good at all things.

Take a look at the diversity of the potential research team. Diverse teams make for better quality research. Diverse teams are more likely to have inclusive screeners, think more multiculturally and be more creative. Diversity and inclusion are not simply boxes to tick or nice features to have. It is imperative and will affect business outcomes.

This is particularly important when you are looking outside your market into new geographies with different cultures. You want a research team that reflects and understands this.

Consider cost comparison

Companies that specialize in your category or segment may cost more. Make sure costs are explained clearly and that they make sense to you. Establishing expectations early can save you money and headache on the back end.

That being said, you get what you pay for. Be wary of companies claiming to be the cheapest on the market to do something that other firms are charging way more for.

Better. Faster. Cheaper. You've probably seen this before. The triangle graphic with a caption that usually reads, "pick two." Most research projects are time-sensitive and yours will be no different. You will want things done well and fast. When you are comparing costs, think back to that triangle. Pay attention to how communicative and responsive the company is during the vetting process. This will likely be indicative of how collaborative and communicative they will be during your project.

Other things to consider

- Will you have a dedicated and experienced project manager?
- Can you meet the company or your project manager in person?

- Do they have any case studies or reading materials that position them as a leader in the industry?
- How long have they been in business and how junior is their team?
- How big is the company (bigger is not always better)?

Once you have chosen your research partner, hopefully you will be up and running with your project relatively quickly, and in the field promptly collecting meaningful data. However, this will vary. If you have given your research partner all of the pertinent information up front and the specs of your study are feasible, the firm could be in field and completed in a matter of days. Is it a tracking (or longitudinal) study? These take weeks to months. We've completed small projects in 48 hours, and had tracking studies that go on for years. If the firm is handling your project from beginning to end, make sure you have given them as much information as possible in the specs beforehand. The more information about your research question(s), your intended respondents, size of sample, etc. you have provided to them ahead of being in the field, the less you will be correcting mid-project, and the less money you will have to spend on those pivots.

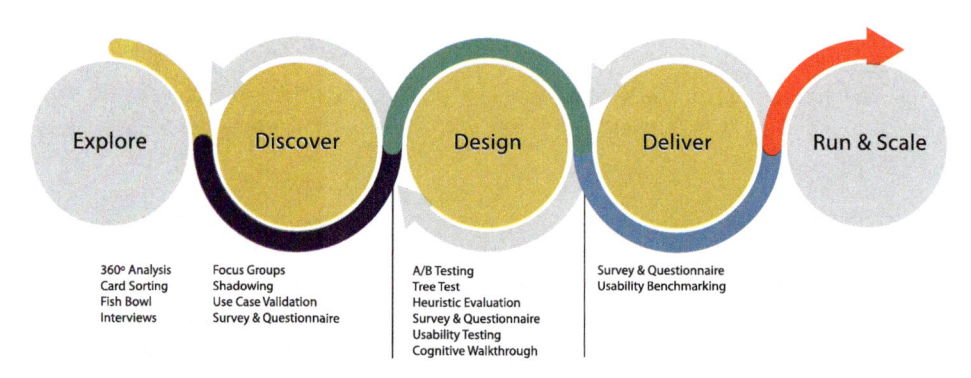

Explore	Discover	Design	Deliver	Run & Scale
360º Analysis Card Sorting Fish Bowl Interviews	Focus Groups Shadowing Use Case Validation Survey & Questionnaire	A/B Testing Tree Test Heuristic Evaluation Survey & Questionnaire Usability Testing Cognitive Walkthrough	Survey & Questionnaire Usability Benchmarking	

If you are working in a region where your native language is not spoken, hopefully you have chosen a research partner that has capabilities to code in-language, and/or provides translation services.

Industry Tip

Insights derived from respondents who are allowed to respond in their native language are more rich and nuanced. Like channel partners, having experienced global research partners is key here.

As the client, you can have certain expectations of your research partners. They are similar to those you would have with any channel partner, business partner or collaborator but they are worth mentioning.

Respectful communication with cultural intelligence should be a given, but isn't always the case. Your research partner should be collaborative and communicative, whether things are running smoothly or there are issues.

Deliverables should be on time, and in the manner they were promised.

Your data should tell a story. You hired a market research company so that you did not have to decipher complex data on your own. You will have given your research partner ample information about the questions you are trying to answer and the data should be reflected back to you in meaningful and actionable ways. That being said, be open to unexpected information. Sometimes this can be the most useful.

OK, so let us assume you have done your research, figured out the right market and confirmed your price points. Are you ready to crack on and sign up some resellers? Nope. Nearly - but hold your horses!

One of the biggest pitfalls is assuming that channel is the right approach for everyone. Let us take a look at where channel makes sense and where it can send you down a rabbit hole.

Step 1

When considering expanding with channel partners, what do you want the outcome objective to be?

Step 2

Create a list of short term (3-6 months) and long term (6-18 month) KPI's, OKR's, targets, goals.

Step 3

Your product and solution will need to be packaged in a way that is right for the channel to sell. This may not be the same as the way you have packaged things up for the direct sales team in terms of:

Content: Do you want channel partners to promote and sell exactly what your direct team sells?

Complexity: For the channel your offer needs to be clear and simple. You can get away with far more nuances and not quite fully baked with direct sales teams. That does not work well for channel partners who will find it confusing to have too many options.

Pricing: Every market is different. It is important to take into account currency and economic considerations. For example if we sell a book in the U.K for £19.99 and try to do the exact equivalent in every country we could be massively overpriced for the local market and are unlikely to sell any. Looking at countries with low Gross Domestic Product (GDP) is a good metric, though admittedly not the only one available, to use.

A country qualifies for low-GDP status when its annual per capita GDP is 70 % or less than the annual per capita GDP of the European Union (for 2023 this means less than $ 27,271.81 US).

Current Low GDP Countries:

African countries

Asian countries (with following exceptions: Bahrain, Brunei Darussalam, Hong Kong SAR, Israel, Japan, Republic of Korea, Kuwait, Macau SAR, Qatar, Singapore, UAE)

Latin American countries (exception: Bahamas)

These countries in wider Europe:

Albania, Armenia, Azerbaijan, Belarus, Bosnia-Herzegovina, Bulgaria, Croatia, Czech Republic, Estonia, Georgia, Greece, Hungary, Kazakhstan, Kosovo, Latvia, Lithuania, FYR of Macedonia, Moldova, Montenegro, Poland, Portugal, Romania, Russia, Serbia, Slovakia, Slovenia,Turkey and Ukraine.

In order to have a good product market fit we would need to look at what price books similar to ours typically sell for in each local market and adjust our pricing accordingly.

This can be a complex issue requiring research so please refer to our guidance on that.

A novice could make significant mistakes by only referring to published statistics or a GDP rating without understanding of the local community or culture.

A good example of this is Africa. The African continent has a land area of 30.37 million sq km (11.7 million sq mi) — enough to fit in the U.S., China, India, Japan, Mexico, and many European nations, combined. Africa is the world's second-largest and second-most populous continent, after Asia in both aspects. Africa is made up of 54 countries with 2000 languages, 75 of which have more than one million speakers.

Despite all this we frequently hear it spoken about and strategized about as one country.

There is broad brush thinking that applies misconceptions and assumptions of a "third world" "underdeveloped", "corruption fuelled" that can be dangerous. This is the reason why we felt it so important to incorporate research into this book.

A great example of this is the smartphone industry.

Worldwide smartphone penetration data shows us that adoption correlates closely to markets with greater affluence. If you take that statement to launch full steam ahead into a marketing campaign you would miss that:

- 46 percent in Sub-Saharan Africa, while smartphone adoption was at 64 percent. This is expected to grow to 50 percent and 75 percent respectively by 2025. Look at regions with potential versus over saturated markets.
- Many people in Africa did not have the same technology evolution as Euopeans and Americans. They bypassed the desktop, laptop, ipad and have gone straight to the smartphone. This affects their perception and expectation of technology.

The number one mistake we see are business plans and globalization strategies that have absolutely no credible research to support them.

Case Study

Gazelle Global facilitated an international project for a major transportation company. In attempting to first manage the study on their own using lists of their existing customers, they encountered some problems immediately. First, their existing customers, while having valuable opinions, couldn't really speak to the business objective of the company. They were looking to expand; to test their feasibility in a new market.

Second, they had no existing incentive structure to compensate respondents/participants for their time. They hadn't thought through the financial infrastructure required nor their capabilities in the unfamiliar market. Something as simple as what currency a respondent would prefer to be paid in speaks volumes about the market, about their potential customers, and about their readiness.

Third, and perhaps most importantly, they hadn't considered the intricacies of a major hispanic market. They were looking for solely Spanish speaking households in a market that was largely bilingual.

We really had to lead the company in several areas, which we were happy to do. However, their desire to skimp on research up front meant this recruit was expected to happen over a weekend. We were asked to correct some of the wrongs they had committed in a time frame that suited their stakeholders.

This meant adjusting our margins slightly. Coming down on the recruit price so we could fairly compensate respondents and execute the work effectively. This is the kind of true partnership you should expect. We understood the importance of these outcomes for the client–they had executives coming to the focus groups and the process needed to be buttoned up. Not to mention worth the money for everyone involved.

Had we more time, perhaps certain big swings they wanted to make in the beginning would've been totally feasible. However we were in the field in a matter of days and managed to provide results to the transportation company swiftly.

What this project tells us about the importance of research and its implications for channel partnership success resound throughout this book but are worth repeating here.

- Have as much information upfront as you can for your research partner. Or your channel partner. Having to make adjustments on the back end with sample or scope costs valuable resources –chief of which being time.
- Culture should inform every step of the process. What are the nuances of your demographic? How are socioeconomic delineations made in the given market? How do those social classes inform the work that you're doing? Spanish-speaking is a very broad stroke. Be specific.

- Be intentional about how resources are being allocated for a given study, and the business decisions that study informs. Are you compensating your partners adequately? Are your partners compensating vendors and participants appropriately? Do the margins you're observing make sense to you?
- Consider the scale and incidence of what you're asking. If general knowledge and a quick google search tells you that finding 500 Filipino neurosurgeons with enough time to complete your 45 minute survey (In English!) is probably not going to work? Don't ask your research partner to find that kind of sample.
- That being said, your research partner should be creative and flexible. If they say no, with no alternative strategy? They might not be the partner for you.

Both Quantitative and Qualitative Market Research are invaluable tools for companies looking to expand, pivot or scale. Coming to a project with this know-how will put you ahead of most.

Benefits and challenges of a channel sales strategy

Let us take a closer look at some of the elements we just covered with the benefits and challenges associated with them for the channel.

Most people only think of reducing the size of your sales team as the benefit to a channel business, but adopting a channel sales strategy for your business has a wide range of benefits.

Benefits

Scaling up

Diagram: Pros of Channel Sales Strategy — Scale Your Business, Local Implementation and Support, Improved Sales and Service SLA'S, Localized Language, Cultural Understanding.

Even if your internal resources are limited, with a channel sales strategy, you will be able to scale your business by allowing your channel partners to attract leads and convert them into final sales. Channel sales partners are able to help by expanding your network, getting you in touch with key clients that you may not have been able to reach with direct sales alone, particularly if those teams are not in your local region.

Even taking into account the sales enablement and training of partners on your products and services on an ongoing basis, channel is still usually a quicker and less expensive path to scaling up and increasing profitability.

Existing Trust

When introducing a new brand to a new market or even sometimes an existing brand to a new market, there is an element of awareness and trust that has to be built. One of the shortcuts of channel sales is that you get to leverage the trust that already exists between the channel partner and the end customer. They are the known entity and their recommendation of your solution gives it an assumed transferred credibility. The partner has endorsed it. The result is savings in time and effort to generate leads and sales.

Ease and Speed

Finding and recruiting a new channel partner is usually easier, quicker and cheaper than hiring and finding a direct sales person. Caveat being if you have something unusual or highly controversial that you cannot find any reseller wanting to sell.

Reduced Marketing Spend

If you are a new brand in a new market the cost of building brand recognition and awareness is considerable and takes time. Partners help you leap frog a great deal of that by introducing your brand straight to customers they know will have the biggest propensity to purchase. In many ways channel partners could be thought of in the same way as we think about investing in marketing that generates leads. I have also seen channel sales sit under marketing departments because of this shared objective.

Market Pilot Programs

When you establish trusted partners a benefit is that they can be very helpful in coming along on the development journey with you and helping test out ideas and give instant market feedback. This might be a marketing promotion, new product bundle, new features or pricing.

Partners can provide feedback, give vertical market expertise, collect competitive intelligence, and are perfect for beta testing and helping to flush out a global product road map.

Streamline your Direct Sales Team

Direct sales often gets dragged down a rabbit hole of a sales opportunity that looks attractive but is completely out of their geographical region or area of expertise. These can be time-consuming long sales cycles. Channel partners are a great source of lead generation and you can certainly have a program that segments certain types of leads so that they get passed to your direct team while thanking and rewarding the partner. Channel sales teams can also be a source for you to hand over sales opportunities that are better driven by a partner to allow your direct team to remain focused on their key objectives and areas of strength.

This can be a fluid arrangement where, for example, once the partner gets the opportunity to a certain stage the direct sales team is introduced back in.

Customer Experience

New customers need to be onboarded and supported with training and implementation. Having local partners, speaking the local language, with the ability to meet in person creates a better customer experience for the initial sale but also ongoing during the sales life cycle. This is important when we start looking not just at initial ARR but on reducing churn and expanding our customer sales value.

Challenges of a Channel Sales Strategy

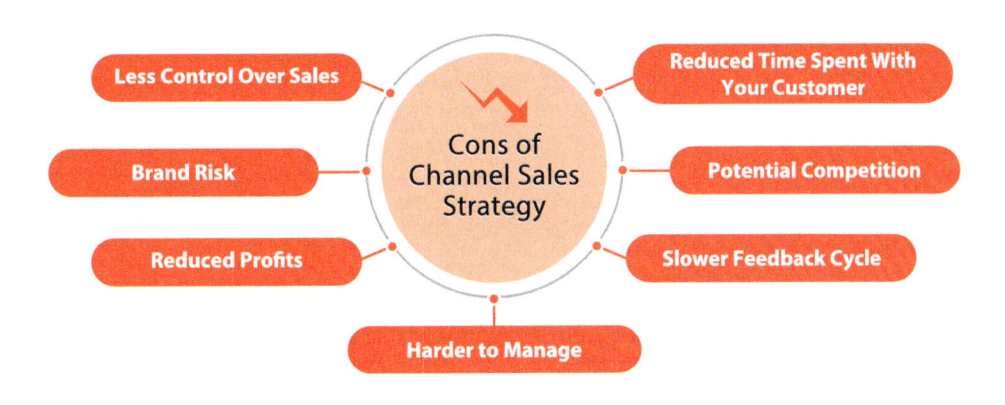

Cons of Channel Sales Strategy

- Less Control Over Sales
- Brand Risk
- Reduced Profits
- Harder to Manage
- Reduced Time Spent With Your Customer
- Potential Competition
- Slower Feedback Cycle

Reduced Control

Listen, these are not your sales people! They are independent entrepreneurs who have successfully run a business and are now agreeing to sell your stuff. They have big personalities and some can be demanding, rude and arrogant all while you are trying to convince them to sell on your behalf.

We find partners will either flat out tell you they do not believe in the potential of your solution yet and will only give a small amount of resources to it or they can nod and then do absolutely nothing. The end result is the same. You go back months later disappointed and wondering why nothing has happened. You cannot control them. You have to win them over with a convincing ROI story and an easy sales process. **High potential low productivity partners are rife!**

Distance

A drawback is that you may not have much control over the sales cycle. Partners can be very protective, not wanting to disclose who the client is and determined to keep you at a distance. This is not the end of the world if everything goes well, but when it doesn't it will mean things that could have been addressed went on unknown for far too long. The best approach is to take partners on a journey and until they have earned their stripes with you keep them close. Collaborate, observe and guide.

Fear

The channel partner's biggest fear is that you will steal their customer and they won't get paid for the sale or that you will somehow embarrass them by letting the customer down for example with a product that does not live up to its description. When partners are afraid they get sneaky. They find creative ways to keep you out and hide information from you.

Understanding these fears helps you to proactively address them and give guarantees that those things won't happen. Talking that out clears the air, shows that you understand their world and perspective and care about the long term partner relationship not just the quick sale.

Pipeline

One of the biggest drawbacks of a channel is that when partners withhold information that restricts your ability to accurately forecast. Most sales leaders want sales forecasts that are no more than 10% out in either direction. This is especially true as you approach the end of a quarter. Having a partner who suddenly announces a large sale won't happen after all or that a large sale has closed is not ideal. Of course the win is better but sales leaders still do not like that as they need to be able to predict, plan and alert shareholders and investors. Therefore the idea of unpredictable revenue will be frustrating. Accurate pipeline and forecasting is a sign of business and channel business maturity.

Brand Exposure

Some partners are complete cowboys and have been allowed to get away with some extremely bad behavior. We once discovered a partner website that looked like it was advertising lap dancers with topless girls on the website with neon flashing lights and, I kid you not, our brand!

Similarly if a partner does not adhere to sales and service SLAs or if you have not mandated them this can lead to a bad customer experience that ultimately affects the reputation of your brand image.

This can have a sudden and long lasting effect on your potential market.

The key is to keep partners close, police them often and be clear about what they can and cannot do by providing them with things like detailed partner marketing brand guidelines.

Pricing

Most channel programs give the partner either a discount or commission. With a discount the partner writes the deal on their letterhead and has more control of the customer because the customer pays them. In this situation it is still important to set some parameters around pricing, allowing a partner to add a certain margin and mandating that they come back to you for approval with anything beyond that for example.

What you do not want to happen is have partners who are selling your solution for double what your direct sales team are or giving it away for free because they have bundled it in with something else they sell, without you knowing. There can be validity in both those things but you need to know and approve. This also reduces direct/indirect conflict as well as conflict between partners in the same region.

Management

In a direct sales team you try to create a culture and get everyone marching to the beat of the same drum. With channel partners each one has their own culture and they beat their drums differently. It takes a specific personality of channel manager to effectively manage partners and handle their ongoing objections of not getting enough margin or lack of product market fit. You are managing multiple personalities, multiple business and marketing plans all at the same time.

Reduced Feedback

You can ask your sales team for a status update daily. You cannot do that with channel partners. Depending on the sales cycle of your product or solution an update every other week is usually reasonable. Even then, as we touched on earlier, partners can choose to keep information close to their chest.

There can also be a hidden agenda when delivering an update or feedback to you. This can mean that feedback is not 100% accurate.

Direct/Indirect Conflict

The worst thing you can do is get partners to generate the opportunity and then decide it is being transferred to the direct team, completely cutting the partner out. It can become very messy for your business when your direct sales team starts competing head on with your partners. For example, an Account Executive opts to remove a channel partner from the opportunity in order to have more control and not have to share the commission.

This sort of behavior can also affect credibility of internal feedback with Account Managers downgrading the quality of partner leads and not providing accurate feedback on their partner leads in order to elevate their own value.

The partner community is often quite close in an industry with partners who have known each other for a long time and are at the very least keeping an eye on each other through social media. If word spreads about partners losing "their" sales to the direct team among your partners in all regions will be suspicious and have a new found reluctance to send you leads. They will go into self protection mode which leads to a reduced number of leads with less transparency.

The damage to the relationship between direct and indirect can be difficult to recover from with each party holding onto the bad feelings. It is well worth exploring how to avoid channel conflict in the first place. We have more on that later.

Developing a Winning Channel Strategy

Great! You have decided that channel is right for your business. Now it is time to plan out a channel strategy. Today organizations that want to do channel right really need to invest in it in two ways: People and Technology. Both should be included in your strategy.

There is no one size fits all when it comes to creating your channel strategy. Products, solutions, partners, regions and your objectives are all so very different. Yet what we often see is a channel manager who has had some previous success with a channel strategy moving on to a new business and attempting to copy and paste. We get it. We all want to get to lying on the beach fast, but it is a mistake.

Similarly we have also seen CEO's read about someone else's channel program and rock up on Monday morning deciding that is the way to go. Just do not do it. It is like that old math teacher (mine was called Allan) that just dug out a lesson plan they had used for the last 20 years. Totally boring and uninspiring, ignoring anything new and reluctant to be creative. Don't be like Allan!

Understanding the diversity of all the elements you are dealing with for your particular business and your particular goals and objectives is where we have to start.

There are many aspects to creating a winning channel strategy. Not all elements of it will work for every business. There are challenges that you need to be aware of and take into consideration when creating your strategy. This will also help you when that CEO rocks up on Monday to respond to them with an educated answer about why you wouldn't recommend that. Explaining why you are not including something in your strategy yet. You will be confident that you have explored all aspects and decided what is best.

Implementing a channel sales strategy requires research and planning. If your business is planning to have multiple sales channels, you will first need to finalize a process that can be rolled out and replicated with each and every partner or channel you pursue in the future. Let us take a look at the key steps.

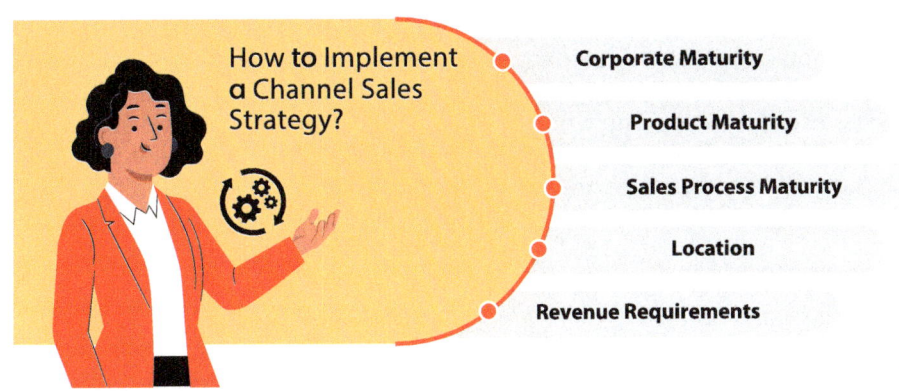

How to Implement a Channel Sales Strategy?

- Corporate Maturity
- Product Maturity
- Sales Process Maturity
- Location
- Revenue Requirements

Make sure you are at the right stage for channel sales

The first step for implementing a channel sales strategy is assessing whether your business has the bandwidth required for the implementation of channel sales and its success. This assessment should be done before starting looking for and recruiting partners. We know that sounds elementary but on so many projects where we are called in to fix a broken channel program this was the issue. They ran before they could crawl.

As an absolute minimum:

- Is your sales process proven and clearly defined?
- Do you have marketing that works to generate interest and leads?

If the answer to those questions is no and you are not yet in an established position there are ways that you can start to work with the channel:

- Find a few partners and be fully honest and transparent.
- Ask them if they are willing to come along on the journey of developing your partner program with you.

Do not try and glue a phooey program together before you are ready. Any partner worth their salt will see right through that. They will either try to take advantage of that or disrespect you or both. Either way it is unlikely that you can turn that around with that partner ever. It is better to wait and get it right or at least have a solid plan, than to dive in and jeopardize what could have been a long-term lucrative partnership.

Good Fit Partners

In our experience it is really quite difficult to figure out proactively from day one who the best and right fit partners are. In most organizations this is simply not as clean cut as strategists would like it to be. It is art more than science.

A great deal of this has to do with understanding who partners are. You will recall from our earlier section that there are so many different types of partner. This means that the personas of the owners and their sales teams are extremely diverse.

As a result we find a better way is to start with a hypothesis which may even be based on looking at who a competitor, or similar vertical market, has as partners. In the beginning we always encourage clients to be flexible and open. Then you see who rises to the top and who does not. There are often surprises and things you just did not know and could not predict. After 12-18 months the picture of who that ideal partner or partners might be becomes clearer. Then you can start to develop a partner profile identifying key attributes.

Some basics to look for:

- Do they understand your industry
- Do they have a network of potential customers that would be valuable?
- Are they a professional operation that you would be proud to have representing your brand?
- Do they represent any other brands and how long have they done that for?
- Do they have appropriate resources?

Example If you come across a partner representing a huge portfolio of 100 brands and they have 3 inside sales people how much time do you think they are going to devote to your product?

Prospecting for Partners

There are lots of different ways to find and assess partners. Usually when we are traveling we have limited time to meet the moist amount of partners. During this time we are conducting a two way interview. We want to know if they are credible and will make good evangelists. They want to know if this product is going to embarrass them in front of their customers and make them lots of money. There are pros and cons to all the ways to vet and we often use different methods concurrently and interchangeably. You need to figure out what sounds like it would work best for you based on what you are trying to achieve, the location and how many partners you are trying to assess.

Ways to consider or rather that are out there. I would avoid some of these.

METHOD	PROS	CONS
Online form. Answers to questions determine if they are accepted.	Quick and hands off approach means a volume of partner applications can be processed.	A form never ever tells you the full story. There are lots of cowboys out there. AVOID doing this and who simply needs volumes of partners anyway? Quality over quantity folks.
Zoom Interview	Quick to schedule. Easier to accommodate multi-country and time zones.	I have been so shocked at how well people can misrepresent themselves on zoom. OK as a place to start but no substitute for an in person assessment.
Group	Create a buzz by promoting to a large group of potential partners. Where a few validate the offering it can help encourage others and get more partners signed quicker.	This can lead to quantity over quality. If used additional meetings should be had as part of the qualification process. The feedback can also backfire if negative resultinging in a whole room no longer seeing it as a viable venture.

Speed dating	Similar to group dating but if you ask the right question you can find out a lot in a very short time. You are getting down to the details and mutually asking what matters most. Setting the expectation of this format is key to avoid appearing rude..	Your memory of partners will start to get foggy after seeing several in close succession. Take notes! Possibly a picture (I always use social media as an excuse for that). it is easy to forget the details or not have enough time to get to a discussion or more substance. Leave enough time in between each one.
1:1 in meeting room	Easier than traveling to each office and less time consuming. Partners also can look more exposed out of their normal environment. They usually come prepared to engage where in their office there can be distractions.	It is easy for a partner to portray that first date polish with talk of success and wins that it is harder for you to validate than if you were in their offices.
1:1 at their offices	This is the best way. You get to see them in their own professional environment and get a sense of where your potential customers might come and what sort of experience they will have.	Time consuming to get to every partner's offices.

Things can sometimes be a bit staged to present a better picture than the reality but this is rare. |

Speed Dating Approach

Unpacking who is credible, who is not fast. When speed dating channel partners, efficiency is the name of the game. You want to be as concise as possible and be able to communicate why you are a great fit in a short amount of time. So the temptation here is to find a meeting room in your swanky impressive hotel (because you want to appear your best, right?) and present to a group of potential partners all at once. The benefits? You do not have to do your spiel more than once and you can quickly get a sense of whether or not people are on board. However, there will always be a naysayer in the group. This applies to almost every room you go into if you are selling something. Perhaps the person has been empowered or incentivised to challenge you. Perhaps they are very apprehensive in general and just want to be validated or reassured. It doesn't really matter what their motivation is. The challenge will discredit you to other potential partners and create a negativity in the room that you then have to combat or pivot from. In that moment, you have lost everyone in the room.

it is preferable to do this one on one. Mind you, you are still speed dating. Concision and showing up as your best self are still paramount.

But let us back up a little bit. Before you are speed dating, you will want to do some outreach. You will assess which of the Partner Personas you are dealing with. There are limited personas and once you have grasped who these people are, you are well on your way to being able to vet them accordingly.

Distributors: This is the manager of your resellers. They are not usually sellers themselves, they are a buy through source. Resellers place orders through them. Some critics of Distributors, often referred to as Disti's for short, believe that they do little to earn the commission and are simply order takers.

Resellers. They could be smaller teams with a few folks rolling up their sleeves and getting the job done by any means necessary. Think of a one-man-band. Or they could be larger organizations with dedicated marketing teams, support and quite sophisticated infrastructure. The persona of the partner here can vary so widely. Resellers may sell in almost every sector or be specialized. They usually have dedicated marketing professionals, employees or external consultants, experienced at launching new products and solutions to their base of customers..

Value Added Resellers (VARs) are a reseller just the same who has a professional services component. They do not only sell the product but they can support the implementation and ongoing support. There are pros and cons to all types of resellers and you should not discount a reseller because they are too large or too small. Find what is right for you and your goals.

> *Tip: There is much confusion around the names that partners give themselves. For example we meet organizations that call themselves a Distributor yet everything they have told us would make them a reseller by our definition. Similarly some partners will say they are a VAR yet do nothing other than sell.*
>
> *Assess this for yourself. It can be a helpful part of understanding what is important to them. In the unspoken hierarchy of partners Disti's are at the top and referral partners are at the bottom. That all comes down to perception and pride. We like to say "forget about fame and focus on fortune".*
>
> *A partner who believes and calls themselves a Disti or a Reseller could in a certain instance be better off being a referral partner to you.*
>
> *Therefore do not worry too much about what the partner calls themselves. Learn what they do and decide how you will classify them. Then decide what sort of commercial relationship you want to have with them right now.*
>
> *This means you could start a Disti off as a referral partner and have a pathway to them operating as a Distributor in the future.*

Independent Consultants. Often with a wealth of experience with an impressive network, Independent consultants have usually worked in a particular industry before deciding to use their knowledge in this self employed fashion. Some can be quite dismissive of this partner group thinking their views can be very nuanced or myopic. We love them! In our experience they can be the hungriest of the partner types. They understand the market, will get up to speed on your solution quickly and have a small but close network they can tap into immediately.

The lack of resources and infrastructure means that these partners can often look great at the start and then fizzle off a bit as they run out of people to ask in their limited circle and are less focused on finding new contacts preferring to leverage those they have. This is not a problem as long as you understand it and indeed can be part of your strategy.

Example:

Short term wins - Independent Consultants. Often happy as referral partners. Low cost.

Long Term Sweet spot - Referral Partners. 20-30% and may offer support services

Fastest root to market - Distributor. 30-40%. Expensive but avoids door knocking to resellers

> Tip: Know which persona you are going after, or if you are not sure, experiment. Go after all of them. Have some hypotheses about what you think might work best but keep an open mind.

With all partners you will be one of many things they sell and will never be their only focus. As a Channel Manager you need to arm yourself with the information about the different types of partner in your region that are involved in the buying cycle. Be confident about the sort of partner traits that would work well for you as well as remaining curious and open to meeting a partner that challenges that.

Channel itself is a cultural shift within an organization. As a channel manager you will have to make informed decisions about which partners to onboard and be willing to adjust if your expectations are not met. This could mean reassessing which partner types are best.

We often find this happens across regions. In one region you have great success with Resellers while in another you have difficulty getting any traction with resellers and everything goes through a well established Distributor. Do not get frustrated if you do not get it right the first time. You will learn from every interaction and be a more informed manager moving forward.

Partner Prospecting

From purchasing a list to cold call outreach there are lots of ways to find new partners. In order to purchase a list you have to have a pretty good idea of the persona of the partner you are looking for. As we discussed in the previous chapter this can be difficult to do especially at the start of a new channel program.

Lists are normally charged based on volume and you may not want to have a broad brush approach but rather and recommended is a more targeted approach.

We like to use good old fashioned cold calling that starts with some desk research to create a list of prospects. Social media is a great source of information. We have seen success with LinkedIn and LinkedIn Navigator.

Example of a cold outreach message

> Hi, Mohammed –
> I see that you are a reseller for ABC. We are a new complementary solution integrated with ABC looking for new Resellers in KSA. Commission is 20% with average sales price of $20,000 and average sales cycle of 30 days. I have a partner webinar next week or would love to arrange a call to discuss more. It looks like you would be a great fit.
>
> Many thanks
> Andrea

Keep an eye on your messaging. If you are not getting responses, change what you are saying. You want to have responses from people that align with the business objectives. Do they sell your competitors' solutions? If they do not have any exclusivity agreements here's where your corporate storytelling comes back into play. You need to believe and convey that you have a better story to tell, about a better product or solution than your competitors.

Summary

You have decided what type of partner you want to target

You have done some sort of outreach

You now have partners who have responded and are interested

Next step is the call to action. Inviting them to meet with you.

Try not to make the partner feel like they are in a sort of audition process. You want partners to be themselves and be eager to explain why they think they are a good fit for you. We always want them to have walked away feeling like they had a good experience and that they could work with you and your company. You want the same thing.

Perhaps the product or solution is not right for a partner at that moment or they have other considerations and projects that mean they cannot move forward immediately. You do not want them to feel dismissed. Either way this is the start of the relationship. Even if they do not move forward an opportunity may pop up and you want them to keep you in mind.

It is not unreasonable to ask a partner who does not want to move forward if there are other resellers in their region that they suggest you reach out to.

The First Meeting

This first introductory meeting should be informal and conversational. Tell them about your children, learn who their families are. This is a two way street. They are checking you out as well. You want to build a relationship here. Make the investment. You will both feel more relaxed. Make sure, of course, that you are adhering to local customs and signs of respect.

Did you know that in the Middle East, which is a vast area made up of different countries and customs that we feel is somewhat done a disservice by referring to it as "THE Middle East" but that is for a different book!

- It is considered rude to show the soles of your shoes like you might do if you were sitting cross legged. Public signs of affection particularly in a business setting would be inappropriate
- In certain regions thumbs up is the same as giving someone the finger in the western world
- Pointing at someone with one finger is considered rude in some regions
- Business cards (and the thicker the better) are still widely used and you should have some

In our experience the people of THE Middle East are very understanding and forgiving of foreigners who make these mistakes, but wouldn't you want to know so you can avoid it? Do your research before you go to any country. Can you imagine if you had presentation slides with the thumbs up and pointy finger on and delivered it all while sat cross legged? Three strikes right there!

Get a sense of the organization chart of the firm you are speaking to. Are you speaking to a decision maker? Ideally you should have sussed this out prior to meeting but sometimes this can be difficult especially if the mid management layer and titles does not accurately explain who does what in practice.

Get a sense of how invested this person is in the firm even if they are the owner. Acknowledge the entrepreneurship of what they have achieved so far. Is this company their baby? This will change how they view you and how you view them.

Ask questions that help to uncover if they have been honest on their website or their marketing materials. Are they really current authorized resellers for all the products they list?

Have they intentionally left some partners or vendors off their website? This will often be because there was a conflict of interest or contractually they have an exclusivity clause and are not supposed to be doing that.

Make sure the partner understands any exclusivity requirements you have so they are more inclined to share whether or not they are working with your competitors as well.

Next, you want to understand who their network is.

Who within that network will be low hanging fruit for you?

Everyone within their network may not be an appropriate target for your product. How will they approach this?

> Tip: You may need, or be better off helping the partner define who that right audience is.

How and when will they reach out to prospects? What messaging will they use? Do you have cobrandable materials they can leverage?

Then, be clear on the next steps. What is the workflow if a prospect is interested? Are they trained up and confident enough to go it alone? Probably not wise at the start. Either the channel manager should support them with this or a warm introduction to a direct sales rep where they can shadow the sales process, listen to the talk track and learn.

> Tip: It is extremely important that channel teams have a close relationship with their internal direct colleagues. While the ultimate goal is to have self-sufficient channel partners, that is a journey and the best people to watch and learn from are your own direct team. A close collaboration with the direct sales leaders can be helpful.

Lastly, and perhaps most importantly (although it doesn't always seem this way), are they going to be nice people to work with? This may seem elementary but, if you get the sense that these people are not going to be pleasant, you are putting an undue burden on your internal team and on yourself. All of these things lead to real business outcomes. Be honest about potential cultural fit mismatches. Perhaps set an expectation that you have some concerns and are still willing to give it a go for 6 months. That way, if your concerns unfortunately turn out to come to fruition, it will not be a surprise to anyone involved that you move in a different direction after the discretionary period. This works in both ways. If you have people that you absolutely adore working with you may be more forgiving when expectations are not met or be able to better resolve down the line.

This information gathering is imperative but you never want it to feel like an interrogation for potential partners. Remember to keep it conversational. This requires you to know your stuff and not rely on notes.

When note taking during a meeting be careful. You want to be looking them in the eye and establishing rapport.

Being able to acquire this information, establish a relationship with the person, be clear about next steps and move forward without any hindrances will streamline onboarding and get your partners selling on your behalf faster.

Potential Pitfalls

Dismissing a partner for the wrong reasons, particularly if the person has come to you. If they believe in your product or solution and believe they can sell it we would always recommend you hear them out. Don't be so obsessed with having a formulaic approach that you miss the human elements which can be full of lovely surprises.

On the flip side, if you keep partners on for too long despite them failing repeatedly in multiple ways, that becomes a drain on your resources and they give you a false sense of what you really have. On paper it looks like you have 3 partners in Spain but none of them are succeeding. You would be far better off knowing that you have a massive gap in Spain that you need to fill.

Engage with the decision makers. Just as with indirect sales this is key. However at VARs and Distributors channel managers can often be allocated to someone who is going to manage your account as a partner vendor relationship. This creates some distance between you and key decision makers. It is ok to work with someone else on the day to day but as part of your partner account plan you need engagement at the higher levels.

If you are speaking to the wrong level of person it can be a very slow and frustrating process to get that information upstream. If you are engaged at the right levels they can help you remove roadblocks and instantly make things a priority. The day to day person you are working with may have their own agenda and may not fully communicate obstacles to leadership especially if it may make them look bad.

Set clear expectations. This is fairly self-explanatory but if you have got a list of things you wanted done by a certain time and your partners were not clued into this list: none of those things are getting done. Did they need a demo kit before they are able to sell? Make sure they have when they need it. More information on demo kits later.

Empower partners with clear goals and action items. Take a look at the kick off templates and quarterly business review templates.

Empower

The goal really is to have your channel sales representatives be almost indistinguishable from your direct sales representatives. It should never feel like you dropped off a cliff or through a prospect to the wolves the minute a channel partner gets involved!

Partners should want to be partnered with you. They should be enthusiastic about it and understand the long and short term value to them if they are successful selling your product.

Empowerment begins with sales enablement (webinars, tutorials, testimonials, product specifications, quizzes and demos will play a big role) which we cover in greater detail later.

There are other rewards that can help you to earn partner loyalty and keep your product front of mind.

- Free accessories or demo kits to help them sell and entice
- Tickets to exclusive events to take key prospects to
- Access to beta features
- Featured in your newsletter or directory
- Partner tiers can create incentive to level up

Your Team

If you are a small operation it is perfectly acceptable to have one channel manager managing the entire operation. As you grow and bring on new partners in new regions you will need a team with a channel manager for each region.

While I have started to see extensive channel enablement roles with up to 20 people on a team solely focused on channel enablement this is not necessary. Channel managers can quite easily wear a number of hats including monitoring and measuring enablement, marketing and events.

The ultimate expectation is that your channel manager grows the partner account and helps the partners with deal strategies to motivate them to perform better.

Channel Strategy Templates

Request PDF's of all templates at globalsaleschannel.com

It can be daunting to have to create a channel strategy. Help is here! We have pulled together four different channel strategy documents that can help give you a great place to start. Of course you cannot use these verbatim but you can look at the sections, tone, format, layout, content and pinch ideas that you think work for you.

Template Channel Strategy #1

This is an example of a simple and more high level strategy we have created for clients than the more detailed and complex board/investor templates that follow. Use something like this to share the overarching vision and to call out key aspects of your plan. Whether you share it or not this should be backed up by a more detailed document that you could direct those wanting further detail to.

Channel Startegy Highlights

Right Partners selling the right things?
Type
Behaviour
Network
Tiers & Pathway
Personas

400 partners. GREAT!
Manage Differently. Prioritise.

Right Process?

Prospecting - negotiating - contracting - Kick Off - expectation - manage - QBRs - Motivating - Variety of Touch Points - New Ideas - Valued Relationship - Sales

Right people doing the right things?
Partner account plans & heat maps
Visits - Bond with individual sales people
Ideas & Industry SME
Wanted. Vendor Days: Food, Training, Swag

Dynamic Partner Enablement

Should not be painful
Bite sized, interesting, use different formats
Individual as well as organisational
Ongoing. Educate on ARR and avoiding churn

Gamification for behavioural modification

Right tools?

PRM integrated with CRM
Research
Standardisation

Internal collaboration
Recognition
Social media for partners

Leadership & Coaching

Transparency, Clarity & Expectation

3 Month Partner House Cleaning

1. This is exactly what we want you to do: Promote & Sell X.
2. This is when: Next 3 months assessment
3. How? Do this. Say this. Use this.

Limit the margin given away.
Partners and our people want to be heard, understood, valued, recognised & thanked

Leadership

Collaborative. Firm. Fast. Decisive.

Evaluate.
Where do you need my help? Tell me what isn't working.
Channel Culture
Copy Best Practice
Clear Channel Team KPIs

No comfy slippers. If I am moving and shaking, so are you!

Key Values: Ownership, Openness & Optimism

Productising what we sell for partners
Simple, clear and quickest path to revenue
Understand partner ROI

Partner Marketing

Don't leave it to them

Provide messaging & templates
Bundle with other solutions THEY sell
Increase touch points. Become interesting and engaging
Plan 6 months ahead so they can plan

Partner Deliverables: Tangible signs of progress
Partner enablement certificates - posted on social
Websites - up to date, easy path for leads
Track leads, update and share pipeline every two weeks
Marketing: 6 month plan of lead gen activities to achieve agreed targets

(Get the right behaviour going & then improve lead quality)

What does 2024 look like?

People: Full of potential. Clear on expectation. Driven. Internally Collaborative.

Priority Partners: Managed, monitored & measured
Process: Professional, clear, easy, trackable, scalable

45

3 key metrics for growth

1. Clean up the basics. Get more from existing partners with existing products
2. New regions
3. New products

Channel $90m of $200m total business representing circa 50%

Estimated goals

	Lead Gen (Later add SQLs)	Sales
Y24	+20%	+10%
Y25	+40%	+25%

Work collaboratively not competitively with the direct team. Some partner leads may go to them. Some of their leads may benefit from a local partner to win.

Timeline

H2 2023 — Clean up

H1 2024 — Expectation setting "Forming & Storming"

H2 2024 — "Norming", increased lead gen, active sales cycles, some low quality leads

H1 2025 — "Performing" - Nice cadence. Able to predict and estimate partner value. Ability to scale well.*

Other metrics

Partner ability to reduce sales cycle

Lead/opportunity quality

Reduce churn and increase YoY deal value

Template Channel Strategy #2

Tip: This channel strategy was designed for an organization quite new to channel. You will notice that many of the sections and wording are designed to not only articulate what needs to be done externally but also to educate internal teams and bring them along on the journey. Adapt this as you see fit and make it your own based on the partnership maturity and understanding your internal teams have.

Channel Partner 3 year Strategy

- INTRODUCTION
- PARTNER PROGRAMS
- 3 YEAR ROADMAP
    - Technology Partners (ISVs, 3rd party developers)
    - Channel Partners (Distributors, Referral, Resellers, and VARs)
    - International Channel Forecast (WIP)
- RESOURCES

INTRODUCTION

Partners are key to delivering on the (COMPANY NAME) mission of revolutionizing the industry's approach to our industry and how we manage humanity's built environments overall.

This best in class technology is a best kept secret unless we let the world know about it. The quickest route to market and international expansion is through partnerships.

Partnerships allow us to:

- Offer a complete solution, addressing the entire build lifecycle
- Scale globally and reach everyone in construction
- Provide bespoke support to global customers

Tip: This ties directly into steps 1, 2 and 3 we worked on earlier.

The channel partner vision is to transform YOUR industry through partnership by building relationships that create advocates and evangelisers for COMPANY.

A Partner-driven approach has been a winning strategy for most successful SaaS organizations. As we continue to grow our Partner ecosystem globally, COMPANY will become more deeply connected to our customers' businesses, continuously multiplying the value of each product and service delivered leading to more efficient customer acquisition, higher customer retention, and increased revenue

3 Months Results

- Established internal processes, created partner portal, partner enablement and launched skeleton program
- 32 approved partners across EMEAI/U.S, 14 Active partners (Submitted sales accepted opportunities)
- Pipeline $229,000 against 17 opportunities. When fully qualified pipeline estimate c.$750,000. Stage 1-2 so values can go up considerably, plus many land and expand opportunities.

Tip: If you do not have any results yet articulate your 90 day plan with a list of deliverables and estimated outcomes. Be as specific as you can. You are asking the business to invest resources and they will want to understand the return.

PARTNER PROGRAMS

While we often reference COMPANY "Partners" as a single entity there are several

Partner Programs, with different objectives as outlined below. It is important to note that there will always be some overlap - a given partner may be part of one or more of these programs. Some of these partner types and programs exist today and some are on the roadmap. However, it is important to acknowledge both current and future state as we plan and build our overall channel strategy.

Tip: Words like channel and partners can often mean different things to different people and in different companies. Do not trip up based on an assumption of the basics. Define exactly what you mean. Here I am acknowledging that this company already has some "partners" and being clear about the difference between that and my program explaining any overlap.

CHANNEL PARTNERS

Current State

Referral Partners: Firms, individuals, and occasionally strategic customers that have close relationships with our target prospects and refer business to (COMPANY NAME) in exchange for a referral commission (5-10% of FYV). Some partners do not accept a commission as this represents a conflict of interest.

Reseller Partners: Reduce the friction of new market entry, by reselling select COMPANY products in key international markets and receive a 20-30% margin on FYV and same annuity in subsequent years providing targets are met.

Distributors: Access to a number of resellers providing speed to market, management, support and marketing. (35-40% discount and annuity if targets are met). Distributors split their commission with downstream by offering resellers who buy through them a commission or discount.

Future State

- ***Addition of* Value-Added Resellers:** A VAR channel builds on the Reseller foundation. These firms can own the entire customer lifecycle from marketing, sales, implementation, support and renewal.
- ***Addition of* Global Systems Integrators:** GSI's such as X, who do not take a commission
- ***Addition of* Service Partners:** Firms that provide additional services to (COMPANY NAME)customers such as training, site captures, business process mapping, staff augmentation, user testing, system integration and support.

Why? Service Providers increase our ability to sell, implement and support globally and ensure (COMPANY NAME) customers are successful.

Who? Many of the Resellers we are already partnered with have the ability to provide services and already do for other solutions.

Currently, all (COMPANY NAME) onboarding is done directly. Our Reseller partner network has the capability to provide onboarding and tier 1 support with an appropriate program of enablement, shadowing and monitoring - this is currently in discussion.

Example: Current pipeline of 3 enterprise opportunities in Egypt. Some previous engagement with these organizations went cold and did not progress. A local partner engaging in Arabic has brought us in with champions and decision makers progressing to a pilot in weeks. English, while spoken by some, is not the language they are most comfortable with. Having this local partner enabled to deliver the onboarding and tier 1 support in Arabic is key.

MARKETPLACE PARTNERS

Tech Partners, ISVs and 3rd party developers that build integrations, applications, or data connectors on top of the COMPANY by leveraging a Developer Portal and APIs. While we do not have these elements in place today, these partners enable collaborative workflows, automate costly, repetitive work, and deliver completely new tools, experiences, and capabilities within COMPANY.

Example: At SIMILAR COMPANY 48% of customers leverage at least 3 integration partners and 85% use 1 or more. SIMILAR COMPANY integration partners include: Company A, Company B, and Company C. These partners can be found on the (insert SIMILAR COMPANY) App Marketplace.

Commercial pros and cons:

- Very few marketplaces have tangible and direct revenue generation.
- Many are logos on a shelf gathering dust with little bidirectional business development benefit
- A dedicated programmatic approach can be successful. Example: 90% of SIMILAR COMPANY marketplace revenue comes from integrations with Company A and Company B, dedicated partner managers for those accounts as well as sales and marketing support. Having spent 6 months bringing on 52 EMEAI integrations to SIMILAR COMPANY marketplace I can assure you that just because you build it does not mean they (customers) will come.
- While there certainly is benefit to Integrations with (insert SIMILAR COMPANY and COMPETITOR) I am not convinced that even with open API's there is enough commercial benefit to monetize and match the level of effort required to stand up a large marketplace.

STRATEGIC/INDUSTRY PARTNERS - (MARKETING LEAD)

Firms that extend our brand presence, help us expand into adjacent businesses, and bolster the value and cost of COMPANY for our customers:

- **Strategic:** Typically firms with global/national brand names that we build custom partnerships with. Within Saas success has been seen with insurance and materials/equipment providers. Here Give examples: SIMILAR/COMPETITIVE COMPANY Partners: Company A, Company B, Company C.
- **Industry:** Provide access to reach members through thought leadership, board/committee participation, influence initiatives, deliver deeper industry engagement outside the COMPANY direct marketing channels. Creates new distribution channels for content and product engagement. Influence industry insights and gain access to business leaders that we otherwise would not reach.
Here Give examples: A, B, C, D

Non profit partners: Social impact program to ensure non-profits have access to COMPANY for their capital projects, which aligns to the COMPANY investment in building community.

These are the same partners that many of our customers invest in for their social impact programs. As we expand into International markets partnering with an International organization such as Habitat for Humanity can be beneficial.

- **Universities:** Social impact program to educate the future leaders of the YOUR industry. Grows demand for COMPANY through exposure to a large user base ~30,000 students across 10 countries, who are the future workforce

for our prospects and customers. Customers value this as our investment in training their future employees and helping fill the talent gap.
Scope International interest - working with local offices and partners to gain insights into higher education programs, professor contacts and build a list of available local resources we can leverage when support is needed.

- **Trade associations:** Prepare today's workforce for the modern jobsite through instructor-led training and on-demand continuing education courses. Reduce friction of tech adoption in the field through supporting training programs.
Here Give examples

- **Minority Contractor/Diverse Business Enterprises (DBE) Initiatives:** Proactively engage with the top minority YOUR INDUSTRY associations to deliver free COMPANY training and develop discounted buying programs. These programs are designed to upskill minority contractors, increase brand awareness of the COMPANY technologies and support our enterprise YOUR INDUSTRY Minority Vendor programs.

- **K-12 programs:** K-12 programs (including high school vocational programs) that provide educational opportunities for the future leaders of the construction industry and training on construction technologies such as COMPANY.
Example: ACE Mentor Program

- **Continuing Education:** Develop certified, on demand education content in line with industry needs and Product Marketing initiatives. Creates top of funnel content to drive awareness of COMPANY's products and services, while further positioning COMPANY as the premier Construction Education provider.

- **Industry Advancement:** Participate in industry association committees, task forces and engage in thought leadership to influence positive change around culture in (insert YOUR INDUSTRY).
This will help to brand COMPANY as a corporate culture thought leader.

The intention here is to give the art of the possible! Ideas about what a comprehensive partner program can include. While we separate out some of these partnerships today and do not have some in place it is worthwhile understanding the menu of options. This connects a partner community ecosystem to our potential customers and expands our visibility of opportunities.

Of all partner types Channel partners present the lowest cost of entry with the quickest return. We have seen this from our early results and will continue to expand on this success by scaling up to support more partner volume.

3 YEAR ROADMAP

PROGRAM	H1 YEAR	H2 YEAR	NEXT YEAR	NEXT YEAR
Channel Partners	• Create Standard global partner agreement • Establish Internal Operational workflow • Source and Implement PRM • Launch partner program in EMEAI • Reactionary partner recruitment	• Proactive recruitment • PRM enhancement (pricing and proposal) • Partner Activation w/ Kick Offs • APAC Strategy • Service partner planning • Develop partner marketing and partner enablement functions • Negotiate and onboard 1-2 Distributors.	• Launch in APAC (6-8 partners) • Launch service partner program • Launch in LATAM (6-8 partners) • Promote referral program in U.S Launch in Eastern Europe • Identify and onboard additional good fit partners in Baltics, North Africa, East Africa, Israel and Turkey. Target 100 partners and $1m ARR • Engage with GSI's	• Start to identify VARS and scope out program. • Identify right fit partner persona • Increase partners across all regions. • Partner with 1-2 GSI's Scale Channel to c. 300 partners $3m ARR
Service Partners	• Identify right fit partners	• Socialize concept internally • Work on a process of discovery • Create a pilot with shadowing, training, monitoring	• Launch Service Partner program to a limited number • Prioritize regions that we find difficult	• Enable Pro Services team to subcontract certified consultants

Channel Partners (Distributors, Referral, Resellers and VARs)

As COMPANY expands globally, capturing ARR from non-Core / ROW markets with greater operational efficiency will be key to success, especially in light of COVID. A Reseller and later a Value Added Reseller (VAR) channel will allow COMPANY to drive revenue from ROW countries more quickly, broadly and with less friction than traditional entry models. This strategy aligns with the following company pillars:

- **Being Global:** Reselling and VAR partners allow for more seamless market entry in countries where proximity, language and network are vital to new market entry.
- **Build for Scale:** There are significant upfront financial and time-to-value implications associated with a Reseller/VAR program. Establishing a program framework and support resources now is key to unlocking scale in 2024 and beyond.

2023 Channel Team Plan

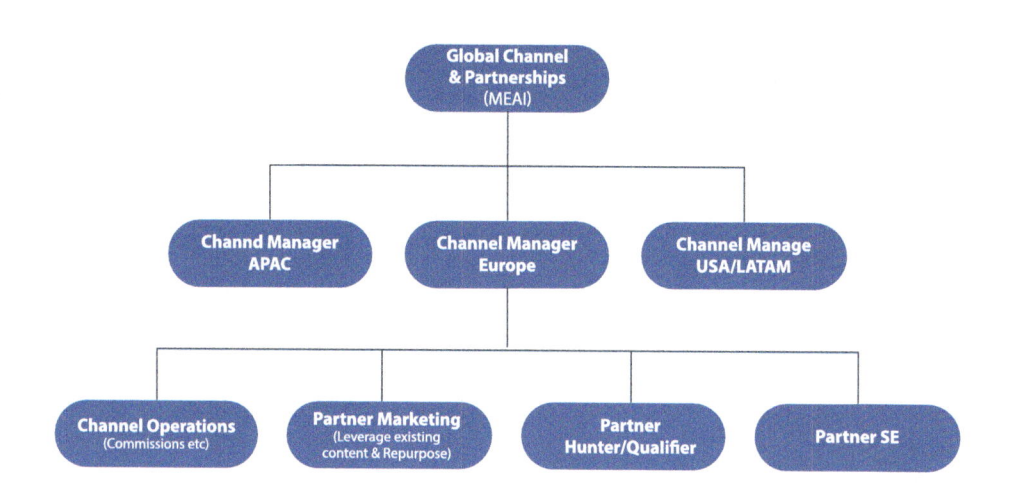

```
                    Global Channel
                    & Partnerships
                        (MEAI)
           ┌───────────────┼───────────────┐
    Channel Manager   Channel Manager   Channel Manage
         APAC             Europe          USA/LATAM
           ┌───────────────┼───────────────┬───────────────┐
    Channel Operations  Partner Marketing    Partner      Partner SE
      (Commissions etc) (Leverage existing Hunter/Qualifier
                         content & Repurpose)
```

Estimated ROI

Still in our infancy with the channel program and indeed as a start up, it is difficult to provide solid data here due to:

New emerging markets - We are in the early stages of understanding how effective productising of (insert COMPANY NAME) is for partners to sell. We may have several iterations of this before we get to a scalable model.

Pricing - We are still working out our pricing models and partners can be sensitive to this

Measurement - Channel is currently responsible for bringing good quality leads to the direct sales team. As a department we have little influence and involvement with the sales cycle. The measurement of channel success must therefore currently be based on Sales Accepted Opportunities generated. While we must work collectively to increase the ratio of partner leads to closed/won this motion is currently largely dependent on the AE/Sales Manager team.

HEADCOUNT	ESTIMATED ANNUAL SAOS	YEAR 1 CONVERSION	MINIMUM VALUE @ $5,000	ESTIMATED COST
Year 1	200 x 3 = 2,400	3%/72	$360,000	
Year 2	400 x 3 = 4,800	5%/240	$1.2m	$240,000 pa
Year 3	400 x 3 = 4800	10%/480	$2.4m	
Closers (opps/SE/Hunter	This team allows us to significantly increase the propensity to find the right partners and increase conversion rates.			$160,00 pa

In the future reselling and VAR partners could own the entire customer lifecycle, allowing COMPANY to forego staffing a full local sales and customer success team and minimizing the

resources required to build an in-region presence. Today Channel partners complement our direct sales team efforts, expand our global reach bringing new logos and ARR.

> *Tip: We talk in more detail further in the book about expectation setting. Expectation setting starts here with the strategy. Sales organizations want instant gratification and while short term results are certainly possible, real channel success takes a few years to develop. Do not fall into the trap of over promising. This will come back to bite you when you start being hounded for, and measured against, results you are not yet in a position to produce well and sustain.*

Partner Strategy Template #3

> *Tip: This partner strategy is a very different style. This company already had an existing channel program that was broken and I was brought in to help fix it. This was more about challenging some conventions and assumptions as well as showing what was possible if we were open to doing things a different way. The audience was different here with a team already bought into the channel program, you will see that the content is shorter and snappier with lots of easy to read bullets.*

Partnerships:

- Distributors
- Large Resellers
- Referral Partners
- System Integrators
- Independent Consultants
- Associations
- Global Systems Integrator

PARTNER	ASSESSMENT	MANAGEMENT	REQUIRED ACTIVITIES	MARGIN	NEW
Disti	Independent advocates, marketing and outbound sales. Communication commitments	"Weekly call QBR"	"Promote quarterly campaign/actions. Participate in incentive programs (to their reps). Attend QBRs and Training"	Up to 40%	250
Small Reseller	Basic questionnaire passed to Disti to assess.	Referred to Disti/Large Resellers	Given access to partner resources. Can achieve badges.		
Large Reseller	Independent advocates, marketing and outbound sales. Communication commitments	"Weekly call QBR"	"Promote quarterly campaign/actions. Participate in incentive programs (to their reps)"	30%	50
"Referral/ Independent Consultant"	Anyone who may come across a lead.	Basic Training. Group Webinars to manage. Self service.	Basic sales training every six months.	"5-10% (Donate to charity option)"	1- 10
Association	Liberal. Looking for large membership numbers. Great brand awareness. Can invite members to be referral partners too.	Regular Touch points including presenting to membership and attending their events. Free educational/ thought leader type workshops.	Agreed periodic comms with membership.	10%	NA
GSI	Accept all	Support with the tools they need to sell us. Regular touch points.	Basic Training.	NA	

Touch Point Partner Calendar

How & how often do we communicate?
15 - 27 Touch Points per quarter
+ Extras like executive intros. Examples: Sarah meets with head of technical/Digital Trans. Adam engages with Larry Silk directly and thanks for business

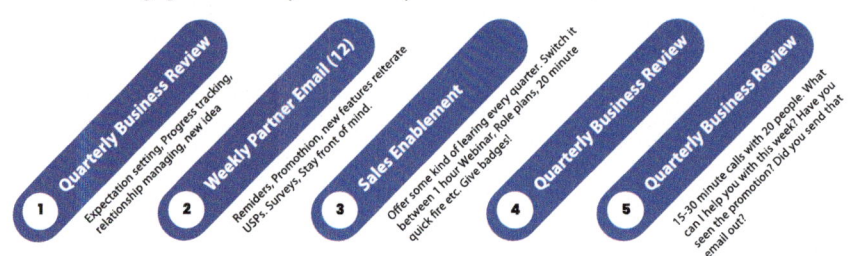

1. Quarterly Business Review — Expectation setting, Progress tracking, relationship managing, new idea

2. Weekly Partner Email (12) — Reminders, Promotion, new features reiterate USPs, Surveys, Stay front of mind.

3. Sales Enablement — Offer some kind of leaning every quarter. Switch it between 1 hour Webinar, Role plans, 20 minute quick fire etc. Give badges!

4. Quarterly Business Review

5. Quarterly Business Review — 15-30 minute calls with 20 people. What can I help you with this week? Have you seen the promotion? Did you send that email out?

Sales Enablement

Introduce Leaderboard & Badges
The channel team is responsible for collaborating with the technical team to create content.

BRONZE	ATTENDED BASIC SALES TRAINING	5 SALES	PASSED COMMON PARTNER MISTAKES TEST	
Silver	All Bronze +	20 sales	Pass 3 silver tests	
Gold	All Silver +	5-100 Sales	Pass 5 Gold Tests	Role Play Pass
Platinum	All Gold +	150+ Sales	Training Host	

Complete List of Peloton Badges & Special Achievement Awards

Tip: Look out for things in everyday life that inspire you and you can carry over to use in or explain your channel partner strategy.
I love the way that Peloton uses badges to motivate me.

Tip: Look out for things in everyday life that inspire you and you can carry over to use in or explain your channel partner strategy.
I love the way that Peloton uses badges to motivate me.

Urgent Actions

Clean up the channel
- 5000 unlabelled Contacts. Tag to enable segmentation
- Reduce partners coming directly
- Partner account plans
- Understand the partner & share internally
- Who do we have relationships with now
- Who do we want to have relationships with
- What are their targets and achievements
- What are the obstacles and blockers

Understanding your audience

Tip: This sounds elementary but is so crucial. Everyone you work with from legal to marketing will have had a different life experience of channel partners. You will too! Just because something worked for one set of channel partners does not mean you can simply rinse and repeat. You have to know not just the company but the culture, the personas and the individual personalities.

Who are they?

20 - 30's

- Varied international backgrounds. Traveling backpackers often end up settling.
- Low base, high commission. Usually broke. Live off Deliveroo!
- Live in small city apartments or shared accommodation.
- High turnover. Make money, learn and move on.
- Sponges! Absorb information fast and via modern methods.
- Sales leaders are focused on building strong, collaborative cultures and creating incentives that not only encourage big numbers but also professional growth, empowerment and a sense of ownership over one's work.

What is Important to them?
- Feeling valued and recognised
- Making money
- Freebies

- Social activities
- Proving to their parents they are not wasters!

How do we communicate with them?

- PDFs are a foreign concept. Think social media. Quick, clear, entertaining.
- Make it worth their while.
- Acknowledge and recognise (to their manager, friends, mum!), thank them.
- Be social! Even if it is virtual.
- Get creative.
- Clear pathway and expectation (gamification for behavioral modification!)

The 3 Partner Buckets - Important things to remember

Distributor

- Lead by sales gurus
- All about sales and ARR
- How can we help them sell more to more resellers
- Hand feed. Say and send this.
- Talk to them: This is hot and this is why you should know about it.
- Talk to them about their resellers: They will love it, send them this.
- Give them what to send to resellers.
- Give their resellers what to send to end users.

Reseller

- Offices full of crazy young sales people.
- Aggressively focused on sales with a catalog of 100+ things.
- Focus on the new shiny.
- Tell them how you can help them sell to the end user.
- Give them what you want them to say and send to the end user.

End User

- Communicating to the end user via the channel is different to communicating directly.
- Pretend we are the partner and speak in their voice, via their culture.
- Experiment with messaging and incentives

Tip: Be careful of your wording depending on the partner. It isn't always "contact us". It can be contact Reseller or Distributor.

Marketing

The role of marketing is not to come up with every channel idea but to work cohesively with the channel team, taking their ideas and content and supporting on brand execution.

Standard Deliverables - Planned in advance

- Quarterly newsletter templates - Channel provides content
- Quarterly Campaign - Hardcopy/printable/on desk piece
- Badges and Leaderboard - Creative
- Weekly Tips and Tricks - Written by channel team
- Calendar of activity - Managed by marketing
- Webinars - Support landing/registration page
- Social Media - 400 Channel posts per year
- Channel Surveys - Once a quarter
- Lists and Distribution - Channel team identifies who, marketing team gets it out on time
- Analytics - Who opened it, read it, used it, generated a lead or a sale as a result

Additionally

- Ad hoc social media - celebrating anything and everything
- White glove approach - 13 priority partners - pick 2 per quarter and do something specific for them

Marketing must be closely aligned with Channel

Hundreds of marketeers. 3 Focused on Channel.

> Tip: In this section I had secret shopped the competition. The company was intimidated by their larger size and sea of marketeers. However take a closer look and you discover that out of all those marketing professionals only three were actually assigned to channel. Much less intimidating.
>
> Marketing must be aligned to the channel. In many organizations, where possible, I would recommend a channel marketing business partner or team member. Marketing to the channel or through the channel represents a very different way of thinking. People with this experience are valuable. However I appreciate in small organizations you get what you can and some...any marketing support is better than none. I think the point here is to be aware. Take

> the time to educate your marketing team about the channel and be clear on where you need their help if they have not worked with your partners before.

Channel Ideas and Opportunities

My 4 big bets:

- New HUGE Distributor opportunity
- Brand Ambassador
- Quarterly campaigns
- Sales enablement badges (use videos) and leaderboard

Your Partners are hungry and eager!

- Collaborate more and find quicker, easier ways of working together. Less email and meetings!
- Can do attitude with a willingness to be dynamic, flexible and if needed reassess priorities
- Freelancers are your friend!
- Amazing talented team and internal resource

> *Tip: You will notice that the language is more casual and there is less detail and more presentation of overarching themes. This was appropriate for this audience. A next step would involve flushing out those themes and providing details. This is only necessary after you have the initial buy in. Sometimes too much detail at this stage can be overkill.*

Partner Strategy Template #4

Last Updated: DATE

Table of Contents

Background

    How We Will Get to Plan

    Key Terms

Strategy House: A Summary

The Mission

The Mission: Why It Matters

Our Goals

    1. Grow Fast

    2. Be Efficient

    3. Be Multi-Product

Our Strategy

    Key Risks

Strategic Pillars

    Pillar I. Win New Capture Customers

    Pillar II. Ensure Existing Customers Succeed with Us

    Pillar III. Invest in a Culture of Efficiency and Decisiveness

    Pillar IV. Scale New Product Offerings

Imperatives: Our Values

Appendix

    Key References

    Financial Definitions

Background

This document's purpose is to provide context to shape our FY21 Partner Plan. This document is intended as a strategy guide and is the result of many and ongoing discussions. It is meant to inform and guide but not prescribe the development of plans to achieve the outlined goals.

> *Tip: This partner strategy is inspired by the W planning process (https://review.firstround.com/the-secret-to-a-great-planning-process-lessons-from-airbnb-and-eventbrite) in which Leadership and Teams across the company collaborate on and ultimately commit to a plan for the year. This is a great way to build your partner strategy by getting buy-in from all internal departments and essentially getting their help to help you build the plan rather than you dictating it to them. This works best for larger organizations with teams of people whose thoughts, feelings, budgets and workload will all factor into the success of your channel program.*

How We Will Get to Plan

STAGE	ACTIONS	KEY DATES
1. Context	Share high-level partner vision, strategy, concrete goals and a starting point for the initiatives we should consider for next year in order to grow the channel.	**Leadership Team Shares Context -** DATE
2. Plans	Senior Leadership team shapes initiatives and presents recommendations on how best to accomplish the proposed goals	**Senior Leadership Team Shares Initiatives:** DATE
3. Integration	Leadership makes final decisions on priorities, funding allocated per initiative and presents integrated plan	**Feedback:** DATE
4. Buy-In	Creation of Department level plans, final refinements and rollup to a unified FYDATE financial plan. Formally launch at Company Kickoff.	**VPs Share Draft Plans:** DATE **Dept Plans Approved:** DATE **Board Approval:** DATE **Company Kick Off:** DATE

Planning Calendar

JANUARY						
S	M	T	W	T	F	S
	1	2	3	4	5	6
7	8	9	10	11	12	13
14	15	16	17	18	19	20
21	22	23	24	25	26	27
28	29	30	31			

FEBRUARY						
S	M	T	W	T	F	S
				1	2	3
4	5	6	7	8	9	10
11	12	13	14	15	16	17
18	19	20	21	22	23	24
25	26	27	**28** *(Board Mtg: Approval)*	29		

MARCH						
S	M	T	W	T	F	S
			Company Kick Off Mtg	1	2	
3	4	5	**6**	7	8	9
10	11	12	13	14	15	16
17	18	19	20	21	22	23
24	25	26	27	28	29	30
31						

APRIL						
S	M	T	W	T	F	S
	1	2	3	4	5	6
7	8	9	10	11	12	13
14	15	16	17	18	19	20
21	22	23	24	25	26	27
28	29	30				

MAY						
S	M	T	W	T	F	S
			1	2	3	4
5	6	7	8	9	10	11
12	13	14	15	16	17	18
19	20	21	22	23	24	25
26	27	28	29	30	31	

JUNE						
S	M	T	W	T	F	S
						1
2	3	4	5	6	7	8
9	10	11	12	13	14	15
16	17	18	19	20	21	22
23	24	25	26	27	28	29
30						

JULY						
S	M	T	W	T	F	S
	1	2	3	4	5	6
7	8	9	10	11	12	13
14	15	16	17	18	19	20
21	22	23	24	25	26	27
28	29	30	31			

Key Terms

TERMS	MEANING
FY24 Strategic Partner Plan (or "FY24 Partner Plan")	Includes the context set within this document as well as other departmental plans.
Channel	Indirect Sales Channel: Distributors, Resellers, Referral Partners
Channel Mission	The high-level outcome we want to accomplish this year related to the indirect sales channel.
Channel Goal	Concrete channel milestones that help us assess if we have accomplished our mission for the year. They are also a yardstick by which outsiders can measure us, including our board.
Channel Strategy	How we plan to approach achieving our channel goals for the year.
Strategic Channel Pillar	A key bet the company needs to make as part of its strategy for channel this year.
Initiative	A distinct track of work aligned to a Strategic Pillar with expected Impact that contributes to Goals and requires resourcing in FY24.
Project	A component of an initiative that will have a specific scope of work, deliverables and timelines and resourcing associated with it

Strategy Summary

Don't want to read this whole document? Well shame on you, it is an amazing read! But if you need a summary to reference, see it all in one image below:

The Mission

10% Revenue from Channel Partners by DATE

The Mission: Why It Matters

> *Tip: In this area articulate the bigger company mission of perhaps selling health and safety software that helps save lives. Why is this important? What value does this add?*

Why does this mission matter?

What's the problem?

> *Tip: Articulate the pain points that your solution solves. This is a high level strategic plan that may be presented to everyone from board members to Investors. While this information will exist elsewhere do not assume they know. Take a minute to articulate what you do and lead into how channel fits into that and the role partners will play in helping the business achieve the overall goals.*

Our key insight

> *Tip: How does your solution solve those pain points?*
> *It is worth starting to introduce here how that is different around the world.*

Where Channel Comes in

> *Tip: How do channel partners support this sales strategy?*
> *What are they going to help the business to do or not do?*
>
> *This may include things like:*
> - *Building brand awareness in local markets*
> - *Complimenting your direct sales team by extending their geographical reach*
> - *Speed to market*

Our Channel Goals

We define concrete milestones to help us assess if we have accomplished our mission.

1. Grow Fast

If we are growing faster than anyone else, and hit a big absolute ARR number, we can feel confident that we will have majority market share in Year X!

- Goal 1: Hit $XM ARR in channel sales

2. Be Efficient

We want to be able to generate the most amount of revenue from the smallest number of partners.

- Goal 2: Reduce channel spend <$45M in FYDATE
- Goal 3: Hit X number of sales

3. Land and Expand

One of the strengths of partners is the ability to identify opportunity. This can mean that the initial value of sales particularly from new partners is low. We must use this and implement a land and expand strategy.

- Goal 4: Double partner sales year on year

Our Strategy

Tip: Here you give an overview with the details of your partner strategy like if you are using a hybrid channel model and if so why.

1. Identify and recruit 20 partners in 10 key "gap" geographies.
2. Broaden the customers' understanding of what we do and how we help them internationally
3. Identify 10 partners that can provide professional services to supplement our customer success team.
4. Position for success against competitors - equip partners for success

Key Channel Program Risks

> *Tip: Be honest about some of the potential pitfalls and things that may not work. This is not always a bad thing. Failing fast can be part of your strategy. It is important to get the buy-in from leadership on that. These are some examples of potential risks but remember to make this your own. The same risks definitely do not apply to all channel programs everywhere.*

1. We are unable to efficiently generate sufficient Partner pipeline to hit the ARR target in the markets we target.
2. Product offerings do not provide sufficient average account value (AAV) to meet Channel partner quotas in the markets we target.
3. Competitors outpace us on features and technological innovations, hurting win/loss ratios, extending sales cycles, etc.
4. Low cost competitors erode our pricing power
5. Unexpected product market fit issues lead to poor sales.
6. Pricing or pricing model is not appropriate for international markets resulting in poor sales
7. Incorrect selection of partners who underperform
8. Lengthy time to onboard and activate partners
9. An unknown unexpected nuance that affects partner success

Strategic Partner Pillars

Our Strategic Partner Pillars are designed to align to our Goals as follows:

GOAL	ALIGNED STRATEGIC PILLAR	LOGIC
	Pillar I: Win New Customers	Adding new Customers creates New Logo ARR
Grow Fast ($XM Total ARR)	Pillar II: Ensure existing customers succeed with us by supporting locally and reducing churn.	Existing Customers can contribute Expansion ARR and Renewal ARR while those under contract continue contributing Multiyear ARR.
Be Efficient (Reduce Spend <$XM, Increase Sales)	Pillar III: Invest in partners who will drive efficiency	This pillar contains partner initiatives that drive efficient spending
Be Multi-Country (Delivers $XM ARR from new markets via partners)	Pillar IV: Scale by expanding in new markets	This pillar contains initiatives to enable partners that help us to scale and evangelize

Each Strategic Partner Pillar has a set of initiatives that most closely align to it in supporting the overall company goals.

> *Tip: Initiatives may contribute to multiple partner pillars/goals (making them even MORE impactful as a result) but we align them to the Pillar of closest match for the purposes of this exercise. Remember you likely won't be able to afford to do all the initiatives and will have to make some choices when integrating them into your final plan.*
>
> *If your company uses RASCI or any other management methodology that can be applied here.*

Pillar I. Win New Customers

To win new customers we need to have new partners generating new incremental sales

What does channel success look like? If only a small percentage of your market uses your product or service (especially if we are used less than a competitor) despite the revenue generated, is that your measure of success? Most businesses want to be the de-facto choice. Google achieved this in Search, Salesforce in CRM, Amazon in e-Commerce.

Success can be measured in a variety of ways. Market share is the gold standard, but in practice quite hard to measure. Simpler metrics are New Logos and ARR from New Logos. The second metric in particular arithmetically ties to one of the Goals. Goals are a good measure of channel partner success. Partners will help us to expand both in the US and internationally.

Aligned Initiatives

Marketing. Partners represent a massive opportunity for new logos and marketing plays a huge part in supporting:

Partner Prospecting

Partner Onboarding

Partner Sales

- Exec Sponsor: NAME
- Risks: Lack of budget, lack of resource to police partner activities

> *Tip: In this strategy every project is assigned an executive sponsor. Internally*

> departments needed to gather executive support prior to including it in the plan and presenting it to leadership. This is a good way to sanity check a plan and save time.

Land and Expand. We know when people try our solution they generally buy it and if they buy it, they generally expand. Can we make it easier to try by empowering partners? We know there are friction points when working with the direct sales teams like time zone and language issues. If working with partners means that we can win new business we will likely get more logos, faster and in the process can also make our sales efforts more efficient. We then have to look at how we grow those initial seeds by having them fall in love with us, trust us and want to expand what they do with us.

It may take a combination of marketing initiatives and product efforts to fully realize this opportunity.

- Exec Sponsor: NAME
- Risks:

Optimize Regions. it is a big world, and international markets are a great source of new logos. We expanded into a lot of regions in FY23, and we have learned a lot along the way. Which regions are successful? Which ones aren't? Of those that aren't: we need to decide what we need to do to make them successful or divest from those that have a critical flaw. To make sure we are being very specific, we will break this into per region initiatives with recommendations for the regions within each area.

- 1 - APAC
  - Exec Sponsor: NAME
  - Risks:
- I.C.2 - EMEA
  - Exec Sponsor: NAME
  - Risks:

Optimize Pricing. Optimizing our pricing may contribute to both adding new logo ARR more quickly (Pillar I) and it may help with expansion ARR too (Pillar II). Key questions to consider: Is our pricing introducing unnecessary friction into product adoption? Are we leaving money on the table for any products or segments? If so, should we rearrange our feature set into product tiers (bronze, silver and gold editions of Capture) or feature-based modules? How can we also optimize pricing for including charging for set up? How might we update pricing to specific segments to account for differences between what pricing might mean for one versus the other?

- Exec Sponsor: Name

- Risks:

Fill the pipe (efficiently). We certainly cannot hit our ARR target without generating about 3X pipeline. Our pipeline will come both from new and existing logos, so this initiative will contribute to Pillars I and II. It also ties to Pillar III in that it cannot be considered successful unless it is in keeping with improving the number. This initiative will be primarily driven by marketing.

- Exec Sponsor: NAME
- Risks:

I.G. Demonstrate Leadership through partnerships. Customers will come to us if they see us creating value-add partnerships that no other player can. This can include those that tie to product functionality or other value propositions (partnerships with lenders that decrease costs for the lendee). To attract new customers we must choose the most impactful partnerships and ensure we can market them well.

- Exec Sponsor: NAME
- Risks:

Optimize Sales and Marketing Efficiency. We must also not forget we generate zero ARR if we do not have happy and motivated reps and a plan that ties to our actual selling motion. In addition, we must design our marketing spend (headcount + variable components) to efficiently build pipeline.

- Exec Sponsor: NAME
- Risks:

Imperatives: Our Values

Our values underpin everything we do and form the foundation for success. We will need to make many difficult prioritization decisions throughout this planning process. Let our values help us along the way.

1. Simplify Everything
2. Expect Excellence from Each Other
3. Done is Better Than Perfect
4. Don't Take Yourself Too Seriously

Appendix

Partner Agreement Templates - Reseller and Referral Partner

Request PDF's of all templates at globalsaleschannel.com

IMPORTANT NOTE: These templates are to be used as rough guides and a starting place, but please check with your own local legal counsel and ensure the wording is accurate for your program and company.

In some roles the legal contract is all the small print T's and C's and who reads all that anyway. In a Channel role you cannot afford to do that. Depending on your seniority you may well have been instrumental in writing it. Regardless if you are in any sort of channel role you have to know the channel contract inside out. This is quite literally what your job is built around. It comes up all the time and you will need to know.

Partners may ask you things like when they get paid and the answer you give will be carefully constructed to be in alignment with and perhaps even referencing that section of the partner agreement.

If a partner does something out of line like using marketing language that suggests they are the vendor, how you ask them to revise this should also reflect that this is a contractual violation perhaps one that could warrant a 30 day termination notice. You will be unlikely to impose that for a first offense but it may be helpful in conveying the seriousness of that matter and that this is something you do not wish to see again.

Know your partner agreement and keep an eye on it for things that may need revising.

Template 1: Short global agreement with page at the end allowing for flexibility, individual partner targets and partner nuances.

> *Tip: This prevents your team going back to legal for every little change. Agree on the parameters of what you are allowed to change in advance.*

These terms and conditions (the "Terms") between the party identified below ("Partner") and COMPANY NAME , ("COMPANY NAME") establish the terms and conditions governing your participation in the COMPANY NAME Partner Program (the "Program"). These Terms are effective as of the date of signature below (the "Effective Date").

These terms create a binding agreement between Partner and COMPANY NAME. If you are signing on behalf of your employer or another entity, you represent and warrant that: (i) you have full legal authority to bind your employer or such entity to these Terms; (ii) you have read and understand these Terms; and (iii) you agree to these Terms on behalf of the party that you represent.

Definitions.

1.1. "Customer Agreement" means the contract by which COMPANY NAME agrees to supply a Customer access to, and/or services in connection with, any Product.

1.2. "Customer" means a third party referred by Partner to COMPANY NAME via a valid Lead Form (that is accepted by

COMPANY NAME) that enters into a written Customer Agreement with COMPANY NAME.

1.3. "Net Revenue" means the revenue actually received by COMPANY NAME under a Customer Agreement for the sale of software Products, exclusive of: (a) sales, excise and similar taxes; (b) returns, refunds, allowances, discounts and adjustments; and (c) amounts attributable to third party products, applications or integrations offered by COMPANY NAME.

1.4. "Products" means COMPANY NAME's products and services that are generally commercially available and described on COMPANY NAME's website at www. COMPANY NAME.

1.5. "Prospect" means a Partner customer or other contact who may be interested in acquiring the Products.

2. Referrals and Obligations.

2.1. Program Levels. The Program may contain rules pertaining to one or more participation levels attached herein as Exhibit A, which are hereby incorporated by reference (the "Participation Levels"). Partner agrees to comply with the requirements set forth in the Participation Levels for the applicable participation level, which may include, without limitation: territory restrictions, sales minimums, professional services obligations, referral fee rates, and other restrictions and obligations. COMPANY NAME may terminate this Agreement or demote Partner from any applicable participation level if Partner fails to comply with the applicable Participation Levels.

2.2. Relationship. Subject to the terms and conditions of these Terms, the Participation Levels, and the completion of all training and certification of personnel as required by COMPANY NAME from time to time, COMPANY NAME grants Partner the right to promote and refer Prospects to COMPANY NAME on a nonexclusive basis.

> *Tip: The matter of exclusivity comes up all the time. Consider what your strategy is now and how this might change in the future. It can be helpful in the early days in a new market to give limited time exclusivity to a partner. If you do that just be sure to update the partner agreement when that changes and not to use the same partner agreement as a template for all partners. You can also leave it here as no exclusivity and issue a limited time exception in the Exhibit at the end.*

Partner shall not sell or solicit Products to any entities, or in any territories, forbidden under the Participation Levels. Partner agrees to (a) promote and solicit orders of Products including, but not limited to the following activities: (i) facilitating face-to-face meetings between COMPANY NAME and the Prospect, (ii) arranging for appropriate Partner personnel to participate in introductory meetings between COMPANY NAME and the Prospect, and (iii) at the request of COMPANY NAME, engaging in reasonable continuing assistance in connection with the finalization of a Customer Agreement with the Prospect; (b) comply with good business practices and all applicable laws and regulations; and (c) market, promote, sell, lease, solicit or procure orders for or otherwise represent any product or service in competition with any of the Products and conduct its business in a manner that favorably reflects upon the Products and COMPANY NAME.

2.3. Compliance with Law. Partner agrees to comply with all state, federal or foreign law(s), rule(s) or regulation(s), including, without limitation those concerning applicable export controls laws, regulations and restrictions of any GEOGRAPHICAL AREA or foreign agency or authority, privacy, data protection, confidentiality, information security, and the handling or processing of personal data. Partner will not and will not allow, directly or indirectly, the use, transmission, export, re-export or other transfer of any product, technology or information it obtains or learns pursuant to these Terms (or any direct product thereof) in violation of any such law, restriction or regulation. Partner shall indemnify, defend and hold harmless COMPANY NAME, its directors, officers, agents, and affiliates against any liability, loss, costs, or damages arising out of or related to Partner's breach of the foregoing sentence.

> *Tip: In this next section consider what your partner sales process is and how you refer to it. In the example below we reference a lead form. Do you use a deal registration or a partner relationship management portal? You can either choose to be vague or specific here which will have pros and cons. Being very specific or only listing one way will mean that you need to amend your entire partner agreement if this changes.*

2.4. Lead Form. In order for Partner to be eligible to receive a referral fee as defined in the Participation Levels (a "Referral Fee") for a Prospect, Partner must submit to COMPANY NAME a lead form provided by COMPANY NAME that has been completed for each Prospect referred to COMPANY NAME by Partner (each, a "Lead Form"). All Prospects will be subject to acceptance by COMPANY NAME in its sole discretion. Without limiting the foregoing, COMPANY NAME will have no obligation to Partner with respect to a specific Prospect (i) if the Prospect is already under written contract to receive the Products from COMPANY NAME, (ii) if COMPANY NAME has been engaged in discussions with such Prospect within the six (6) months prior to receipt of a Lead Form from Partner for such Prospect, or (iii) if Partner fails to meet its obligations under Section 2.2 with respect to such Prospect. Each Lead Form will automatically expire one-hundred twenty (120) following receipt thereof by COMPANY NAME unless separately agreed in writing by COMPANY NAME.

2.5. Right to Change Price and Product. COMPANY NAME reserves the right to set and change prices of, or change or modify the design of or discontinue, any of the Products at any time or to add Products at any time, including any territory-specific pricing. Partner understands that COMPANY NAME is not bound to any price (whether or not on any then-current price list) with respect to a Prospect until it has entered into a Customer Agreement, and Partner will not imply or represent anything to the contrary to any person or entity. Any software is licensed and not sold; any references herein to the sale or price of any software or any copy thereof refers to the license or license fee thereof.

2.6. Independent Contractors. The parties are independent contractors and not partners, joint venturers or otherwise affiliated and neither has any right or authority to bind the other in any way. Accordingly, Partner shall not commit COMPANY NAME to any Customer Agreement or other contract or obligation.

> *Tip: This legal language can be confusing so make sure it applies to your situation. Independent Contractors can be referral or reseller partners just like the others. Here it would be helpful to have a definition of what you mean by Independent Consultants so that you do not end up telling a whole group they cannot do something when that is not really what you mean.*

2.7. Channel Partners may not engage sub-tiers of distributors, resellers, integrators or other representatives without, in each case, first obtaining written consent from COMPANY NAME, in its sole discretion.

3. Referral Fees. During the term of these Terms, for each Customer Agreement executed by COMPANY NAME and a Customer, COMPANY NAME will pay to Partner a Referral Fee as set forth in the Participation Levels. Unless otherwise set forth in the Participation Levels, or agreed in writing by COMPANY NAME, the Referral Fee is equal to the product of (i) the referral fee percentage set forth in the Participation Levels and (ii) all Net Revenue actually received by COMPANY NAME in respect of such Customer Agreement during the twelve (12) months following execution of such Customer Agreement, provided Partner complied with all of the terms and conditions herein.

4. Ownership. As between the parties, COMPANY NAME owns all right, title and interest in and to the Products including any trademark, services marks or trade names used in connection with the Products.

> *Tip: Adapt this for your situation depending on if you are giving partners referral fees, commission or discounts.*

5. Warranties: Disclaimer.

5.1. Warranties. Any warranties for the Products shall run directly from COMPANY NAME to the Customer or Prospect. In no event shall Partner make any representation, guarantee or warranty concerning the Products, or terms and conditions of any Customer Agreement, except as expressly authorized in writing by COMPANY NAME. Partner shall indemnify, defend and hold harmless COMPANY NAME, its directors, officers, agents, and affiliates against any liability, loss, costs, or damages arising out of or related to Partner's breach of the foregoing sentence.

5.2. Disclaimer. COMPANY NAME MAKES NO WARRANTIES TO PARTNER, EXPRESS OR IMPLIED, AND HEREBY SPECIFICALLY DISCLAIMS ALL IMPLIED WARRANTIES OF MERCHANTABILITY, NON-INFRINGEMENT, AND FITNESS FOR A PARTICULAR PURPOSE, AND ALL WARRANTIES ARISING OUT OF USAGE OR TRADE, COURSE OF DEALING AND COURSE OF PERFORMANCE.

6. Liability Limitation. EXCEPT WITH RESPECT TO A BREACH OF APPLICABLE LAW OR BREACH OF CONFIDENTIALITY OR INTELLECTUAL PROPERTY RIGHTS, NEITHER PARTY WILL BE LIABLE OR OBLIGATED WITH RESPECT TO ANY SUBJECT MATTER OF THIS AGREEMENT OR UNDER ANY CONTRACT, TORT, STRICT LIABILITY OR OTHER LEGAL OR EQUITABLE THEORY, WHETHER OR NOT ADVISED OF THE POSSIBILITY OF SUCH DAMAGES WHATSOEVER, FOR ANY (I) SPECIAL, INDIRECT, INCIDENTAL, EXEMPLARY, PUNITIVE, RELIANCE OR CONSEQUENTIAL DAMAGES, INCLUDING LOSS OF PROFITS, REVENUE, DATA OR USE, AND (II) ANY LIABILITY IN EXCESS OF THE REFERRAL FEES PAID AND PAYABLE BY COMPANY NAME TO PARTNER DURING THE TWELVE (12) MONTHS PRIOR TO THE EVENT GIVING RISE TO SUCH LIABILITY.

7. Term and Termination.

7.1. Termination. Either party may, at its option, terminate these Terms upon thirty (30) days' written notice to the

other party for any reason or for no reason whatsoever. These Terms may also be terminated by either party upon five (5) days' written notice if the other party breaches these Terms in any material respect and the breaching party fails to cure such breach within such 5-day period.

> *Tip: There are certainly more lengthy and complex cancellation periods to be found in partner agreements. However, we tend to think if the worse case happened and we needed to get out of this partner agreement how long with that take us in every scenario. Here you have a standard 30 days and an emergency 5 days. Organizations with longer termination periods tend to be thinking about information or relationships or potential sales the partner might be working on and how not to lose all that. We tend to be more concerned about if they are doing something unethical or illegal and how quickly we would want to get out of that!*

7.2. Effect of Termination. Upon any termination or expiration of these Terms, Partner shall immediately cease all promotion of the Products and shall immediately return to COMPANY NAME, or at the option of COMPANY NAME, destroy, all Confidential Information of COMPANY NAME, and Products provided to Partner hereunder; and COMPANY NAME may market, sell or provide the Products to any third party, without obligation to pay Partner any Referral Fees. Notwithstanding any termination or expiration of these Terms, COMPANY NAME agrees to pay all Referral Fees earned by Partner prior to termination, and the following Sections shall survive and remain in effect: 1, 4, 5, 6, 7.2, 8 and 9. Any termination or expiration of these Terms shall be without prejudice to any other rights or remedies available under these Terms or at law.

8. Confidentiality. Partner acknowledges that, in the course of performing its duties under these Terms, it may obtain business, technical or financial information relating to COMPANY NAME, all of which is confidential and proprietary ("Confidential Information"). Confidential Information shall include, without limitation, all of COMPANY NAME's customer lists and information relating the Products, pricing and any related services. Partner and its employees and agents shall, at all times, both during the term of these Terms and after its termination, keep in trust and confidence all such Confidential Information, and shall not use such Confidential Information other than in the course of its duties as expressly provided in these Terms; nor shall Partner or its employees or agents disclose any Confidential Information to any person without COMPANY NAME's prior written consent. Partner will not be bound by this Section with respect to information it can document (i) has entered or later enters the public domain as a result of no act or omission of Partner, or (ii) is lawfully received by Partner from third parties without restriction and without breach of any duty of nondisclosure by any such third party. If required by law, Partner may disclose Confidential Information, provided Partner gives adequate prior notice of such disclosure to COMPANY NAME to permit COMPANY NAME to intervene and to request protective orders or other confidential treatment therefore. Partner acknowledges and agrees that all records regarding Customers shall be considered COMPANY NAME Confidential Information, and shall not use any such records except promotion of COMPANY NAME Products under these Terms.

9. Miscellaneous.

> *Tip: One of the biggest redlining time delays we see is when an American headquartered company starts doing business outside of the U.S yet all the laws referenced and the court you have to go to if the dodo hits the fan are in the U.S. This is really quite outdated and annoyed partners from the start. You are partnering with a Reseller in Dubai but they will have to fly to San Francisco if there is a problem? More knowledgeable partners will not sign something like that and will be somewhat offended that it is in there at all. The wording below is more mindful of this acknowledging local laws. Your ability to do this and how you word it may depend on where you have registered offices so definitely need to check in with your local legal counsel.*

9.1. Choice of Law. If your principal place of business is located in the GEOGRAPHICAL AREA, these Terms will be governed by and construed in accordance with the laws of the GEOGRAPHICAL AREA, without regard to the provisions of the conflict of laws thereof, and any action, claim, dispute or proceeding arising out of or relating to these Terms shall be brought exclusively in the courts sitting in GEOGRAPHICAL AREA. If your principal place of business is located outside the GEOGRAPHICAL AREA, these Terms will be governed by and construed in accordance with the laws of GEOGRAPHICAL AREA, without regard to the provisions of the conflict of laws thereof, and any action, claim, dispute or proceeding arising out of or relating to these Terms shall be brought exclusively in GEOGRAPHICAL AREA.

9.2. Notices. Any notice or other communication required or permitted in these Terms shall be in writing and shall be deemed to have been duly given (i) on the day of service if served personally, (ii) upon receipt if mailed by First Class mail, registered or certified, postage prepaid, and addressed to the respective parties at the addresses set forth above, or at such other addresses as may be specified by either party pursuant to the terms and provisions of this section, or (iii) upon written acknowledgement of receipt, if sent via email to the email .

9.3. Assignment. Partner may not subcontract, delegate, assign or otherwise transfer any rights or obligations under these Terms without the prior written consent of COMPANY NAME. Any attempt to do otherwise shall be void and of no effect.

9.4. Severability. Any provision of these Terms that is determined to be unenforceable or unlawful shall not affect the remainder of the Agreement and shall be severable therefrom, and the unenforceable or unlawful provision shall be limited or eliminated to the minimum extent necessary to that these Terms shall otherwise remain in full force and effect and enforceable.

9.5. Entire Agreement. These Terms (together with all attachments and exhibits hereto) constitutes the entire agreement between the parties and supersedes any and all prior agreements between them, whether written or oral, with respect to the subject matter hereof. These Terms may not be amended, modified or provision hereof waived, except in a writing signed by the parties hereto. No waiver by either party, whether express or implied, of any provision of these Terms, or of any breach thereof, shall constitute a continuing waiver of such provision or a breach or waiver of any other provision of these Terms.

IN WITNESS WHEREOF, intending to be legally bound, the parties have caused their duly authorized officers to execute these Terms as a sealed instrument, as of the Effective Date.

[Add Signature for partner and Company]

> TIP: When scaling up your channel program standardization is key. However it can be really difficult to come up with one agreement that works for every partner everywhere. Going back to legal every time you need a change is time consuming, expensive and a pain in the butt. We like to suggest the addition of an Addendum or here "Exhibit A" which:
> - Keep the bulk of your contract that legal has approved the same for everyone.
> - Acknowledges the need for some flexibility and allows channel managers or Channel Directors or Operations (someone other than legal - you decide based on how you work) to make some partner specific changes
> - Enables speedier contract negotiations
>
> For this to work after your standard agreement is created come up with internal agreement on what can be approved outside of legal and who can do that. In the example below you can see that you can:
> - Alter the expectation setting a specific job description for that partner
> - Change the targets and commission
> - Alter the training and service SLAs
>
> We like this approach too because in addition to speed it gives channel managers some ammunition "Sorry these things are part of our standard partner agreement. I cannot change those. However I can customise these areas so we address your concerns".

EXHIBIT A

Partner Type: Reseller

Expectation: Resellers will qualify, demo and process opportunities being self-sufficient utilizing tools provided.

Commission/Discount:

- 20% discount . Total annual subscription payable to COMPANY NAME within 30 days of PO.
- Target: No target for 12 months

Required Training: Gold Level.

Product Focus: Capture only. Track upon approval.

Professional Services: Must have ability to provide onboarding and first level support upon approval from COMPANY NAME to do so.

Pipeline: Bi-weekly pipeline updates with Regional Sales Managers.

Pricing: End User pricing to be approved by COMPANY NAME and copies of all user pricing agreements provided.

COMPANY NAME adheres to international privacy laws including GDPR. The COMPANY NAME privacy policy is found here: https://www.COMPANY NAME.

> Tip: One of the things missing from this partner agreement but often asked for is your timeline to pay partners. In this instance it was deliberately missing because we had not figured it out yet. More sophisticated partners will ask for this .This is an important point that actually requires quite a bit of work and cross departmental collaboration in the background. How long does the validation of the sale and internal reconciliation of the partner payment take?

PARTNER	ASSESSMENT	MANAGEMENT	REQUIRED ACTIVITIES	MARGIN	NEW
Disti	Independent advocates, marketing & outbound sales. Communication commitments	Weekly call QBR	Promote quarterly campaign/actions Participate in incentive programs (to their reps), Attend QBRs & Training	Up to 40%	250
Small Reseller	Basic questionnaire passed to Disti to assess.	Referred to Disti/Large Resellers	Given access to partner resources. Can achieve badges.		
Large Reseller	Independent advocates, marketing & outbound sales. Communication commitments	Weekly call QBR	Promote quarterly campaign/actions Participate in incentive programs (to their reps)	30%	50
Referral/ Independent Consultant	Anyone who may come across a lead.	Basic Training. Group Webinars to manage. Self service.	Basic sales training every six months.	5-10% (Donate to charity option)	1- 10
Association	Liberal. Looking for large membership numbers. Great brand awareness. Can invite members to be referral partners too.	Regular Touch points including presenting to membership & attending their events. Free educational/th ought leader type workshops.	Agreed periodic comms with membership.	10%	NA
GSI	Accept all	Support with the tools they need to sell us. Regular touch points.	Basic Training.	NA	

Template 2: IN PRINCIPLE DISTRIBUTION AGREEMENT

> *Tip: You have found a distributor that you want to work with. If you just send them a legal agreement it is likely to get redlined to death. I like to send an in principle agreement to check we agree on things and then send that to legal to get incorporated into a legally binding contract.*
>
> *This speeds things up and is often easier to work with. It allows both sides to speak real English and not get tied up in legalese.*

This is a working document in lieu of a legal contract intended to give partners an understanding of

the strategic plan for COMPANY Channel.

COMPANY is a simple product designed to serve the construction industry and solve a simple problem. As such we have kept the pricing model and sales process simple too. We intend to follow this approach with our channel strategy.

Structure

- Hybrid Partners
- Resellers
- Referral Partners

Pricing

COMPANY has two ways of pricing:
a) Project price - using the project construction volume
b) Bundle price

One subscription price includes remote implementation and support.
Average Sales Price $16,000

Commission

Paid on the first year's invoice. This includes any upgrades within the first year.

Professional Services

Implementation - This is a simple 30 minute remote meeting. This will be done by the Reseller.

An additional menu of services that partners can offer locally with accompanying training represent

additional revenue opportunities.

Bidirectional partnership

Partner services will be promoted to COMPANY direct customers. Partners will deliver value in:

- Product adoption and expansion
- Onsite support
- Local Language and cultural understanding

Workflow

1. End user identified
2. Partner gives overview & demo
3. Partner accesses pricing calculator on PRM
4. Partner submits proposal to customer
5. Partner Professional services - contracted directly with customer
6. Customer signs using docusign to accept
7. COMPANY activate account
8. Partner delivers implementation training in person or online
9. Customer relationship transferred to COMPANY Customer Success for ongoing management
10. Partner handle level one troubleshooting
11. Expansion opportunities explored
12. Partner commission processed upon receipt of customer payment and signed contract

Logistics

No geographical territories or exclusivity.

- COMPANY wants to minimize the number of partners transacting with us directly. Where possible partners will be referred to work via Distributor. However, there will be instances where a Reseller works directly with COMPANY.
- PRM allows partners and COMPANY to see progress of each opportunity.
- We prefer end user contracts to be directly with COMPANY but have the ability for Partners to contract directly where this makes sense.

- Where possible we allow payments in local currency.

Timeline

We intend to go live with the launch of our channel program in January 2024 with a view to having the major tools in place by March 31st.

At this point we will have our major Distribution partnerships in place and the launch/target will be reseller/referral partners with the aim of building regional brand awareness.

Marketing

- COMPANY has an impressive catalog of marketing covering social media, print and events. The Channel will leverage this in 2024.
- Brand Ambassadors - Identifying regional champions who will produce complementary content and help build the brand locally in lieu of local case studies

Training

Courses Partner Service Level Requirement

> *Tip: Here provide a breakdown of what the training requirements will be both for the distributor as well as any of their resellers. Note if it is different or the same for all partner types.*

Upon completion partners receive an associated service level certificate and badge which can be used on websites and in collateral.

Please share your thoughts on the plan so far.

Supporting Internal Teams

Channel is still often considered as one of those business partners that is outside the main group of functions. More a nice to have than a necessity. As a Channel team one of your main jobs (yes we said main) will be to make sure that as well as educating your partners which we will come on to in the end chapter, it is extremely important to have a collaborative approach with eternal teams, gently educating them and keeping them informed.

Current State

- Understand what different departments know about the channel. Have they worked successfully with channel programs in the past?
- Are they used to channel programs that will be quite different to yours such as giant sophisticated resellers versus small ma and pa resellers?
- Has the business already had some experience with partners and if so understand the history, the effect on different departments and individuals

Planning

Consult with each department and individuals within at the idea stage. Can you simply write your plan, launch it and chuck it at them? Of course you can but expect to be met with resistance and resentment.

Run your ideas by them being open to feedback and encouraging people to share obstacles. We like to say "tell us what we are missing".

Internal Channel Wiki

This is an internal web page. In a lot of organizations different departments will have one and channel should too.

- Articulate what you mean by partners
- Post guides on how to work with partners
- Provide links to all forms and resources in one place clearly labeled
- Share your strategy being open and transparent
- Allow for anonymous submissions of things that are not working or driving them mad
- Meet your channel partners - post videos of partners
- Testimonials - win stories highlighting successful partner sales or collaboration

This is a combination of your internal sales tool as well as a resource center and one stop shop for all things channel.

Example of internal channel wiki page

Be approachable and accessible

We often think of this as just something that we need when working with partners externally but it is equally as important when working with internal teams. You need them and in order to get their support you have to understand them, create space for them to comfortably share concerns and listen.

Having a periodic recurring informal virtual channel coffee hour is a really useful tool for this. People may not share what they really really think in large or more formal groups.

Taking the time to attend departmental team meetings and giving a presentation with lots of time to answer questions is valuable. This should be something that you build on. Perhaps on a next visit play a video of a partner or do a live call and introduce a team to them who would otherwise not normally come into contact with partners.

Here is a real example of the questions we received when we were launching a channel program internally. As you can see you need to know your program inside out and be prepared for anything.

Channel Partner Program FAQs- Educating Internal Teams

Question: How do you address the concerns from partners that we will eventually go direct ourselves after they invested so much? Or if we have both direct and indirect sales in a region?

Answer: Great question.

Partners are part of our overall international growth strategy.

Our intention is to leverage partners and in fact expand the value of partners through the professional services they can bring from customer onboarding to additional value adds like site capture or support around COMPANY NAME integration. It is unlikely our own internal resources will be able to cope with that demand.

Our goal is to generate as much new business as possible in the region. Alienation of a partner community which would then cut off a stream of business which we anticipate will yield a higher global value than our direct business is simply not in our best interest.

We are following the business models of other successful industry players (give examples here that relate to your industry.) 70% of revenue from partners like X and X has 300+ partners. X who canceled their channel program saw a slump in business and have lost their market share. We know that the use them and ditch them approach has not been successful.

This last point depends on if you are offering this or not: A partner's ability to have annuity on the customer for the next 2,3 years and possibly longer is tangible and indicative of our long term commitment to partners.

Referral programs often raise suspicion around this. Organizations with no real long term partner strategy usually do light weight referral rather than reseller/ Disti. Showing we have a whole global channel strategy and team, that we have made massive investments in tools like our PRM ($50K per year) is all indicative of long term commitment to partners.

Question: What if they ask if they can be exclusive? If they are concerned about multiple partners in one region?

Answer: They all ask that. We do not offer any exclusivity. As an early partner they are in a great position to get submitting leads and have their name tagged to them. We do not know how productive a partner will be.

What we can do Mr Partner is offer you exclusive opportunities (trade shows, print ads, spiffs) in exchange for new business from you.

Question: Hi Andrea, what do you think of a customer that has a subsidiary that wants to be our channel partner? Any caveats here?

Answer: Not many.

If they get a demo org they could figure out a way to use that for their needs rather than pay us. For the most part they know our solution first hand and make a great advocate.

I have run campaigns encouraging this. "Send us 5 customers and that pays for your subscription".

Question: What if they want to be a more official channel partner? Not just a referral?

Answer: Same applies. No concern.

Question: If it is our inbound leads, do we usually pass to our reseller? If so, do they still get the same margin?

Answer: This is an option. The answer to both could be yes. Several considerations including if we believe the partner is worth it. I would usually have some sort of prove yourself to me period before rewarding them with this.

Question: Do we ever disclose our financial info to resellers if they asked for it?

Answer: Yes. Partnership is often a two way street. So the partner can reasonably want to ensure the stability of our company before they invest in partnering with us. I would point them to publicly available information.

Question: Is the reseller signing an agreement directly with customers or do we sign directly with customers? What if there are currency and tax issues?

Answer: Customers should sign directly with the Company. That does not mean that the commercial arrangement has to happen directly with the Company.

I flagged the taxes and currency issue with finance. My suggestion was to create an account with Payoneer (Tip: great software for any channel managers struggling with multi currency) . This is inexpensive and simple to do and resolves this issue instantly.

Question: Customer has a subsidiary that wants to be our channel partner?

Answer: More information required. In principle the answer could be yes. Would need to understand more about the potential value versus any risks. Sometimes things like this must be looked at on a case by case basis rather than applying a programmatic approach.

Question: Does our partner portal support different languages and provide training?

Answer: Yes to both. I have sent you a video and overview document that you might find helpful.

Question: Can we have pricing calculators for channel partners on the partner portal?

Answer: The software has this capability. We are currently building this out.

Question: Customer wants to be our channel partner.

Are they opportunistic or do they have more structure in business development and investment in the company? Even opportunities, how often?

Answer: Valid points and questions. Can sometimes work. I would look at this on a case by case basis.

Question: Who should be managing resellers? AE or channel managers?

Regional channel managers, the AE should only be coming for specific opportunities.

Answer: Correct. The channel team should manage channel partners.

Question: Under our current referral agreement, do we pay them for additional deals if they refer us to a new customer within the contract period (12 months), also what about the renewal.

Answer: A referral partner gets paid for each new logo they bring in that we close/win.

The partner gets paid on the first year's annual invoice.

Renewals or annuity is used as a carrot in the channel. In EMEAI and LATAM Resellers who achieve aggressive targets are rewarded with annuity in years 2 and 3.

Onboarding

Sales Enablement for Channel Partners

Staying front of mind by engaging with your channel partners- even if it is not with business intentions in mind. Communicate with them.

Think about the onboarding process for internal sales teams. Quite often larger firms and tech companies send people to a training center in some wonderful part of the world. You've got their dedicated attention for a week or sometimes two. you are winning and dining them, giving them all sorts of goodies and creating a fantastic onboarding experience. When it comes to partners, they usually get an online portal, a webinar and maybe a branded Polo shirt and off they go.

The experience is completely different and so is your ability to attain and maintain their attention. Research around learning and development, particularly in a remote environment, overwhelmingly shows that we respond better to small, bite-sized chunks of information that is delivered in varied forms. Don't just present a PDF, for instance, but include a PowerPoint, a video, a short survey or quiz. Maintain the seller's attention by keeping them engaged and entertained. What's more, stay front of mind by engaging with your channel partners even if it is not with business intentions in mind. Communicate with them. Have a kick off call with channel partners after training. Make sure they feel prepared and have what they need to be successful. Remind them that there is a living breathing entity behind the training modules and contracts: Your company.

Corporate storytelling is a vastly undervalued and underestimated resource in onboarding and working with partners. When it comes to engagement and persuasion, nothing works better than a story. When you are an experienced sales person you have got countless stories. You've been through it, you have seen it all, you have examples of customers - what worked, what did not and where the ROI was: particularly if you have been with one company for a long time. Partners do not have this luxury. They do not have the talk track ready to go. So we need to hand it to them.

Research indicates that we are much more likely to remember a story than facts and figures. Presenting information to partners, and thus the prospects they come in contact with, in narrative form will serve to keep you and your product top of mind.

Teaching Partners to use Corporate Storytelling:

1. Relate the narrative to them. "You know, I worked with a company just like yours: it was a small accounting firm. They would receive boxes and boxes of invoices from independent tradespeople - one-man-band types. There was a literal shoebox of receipts. People had to painstakingly go through each receipt and manually enter the figures. They did not think there was

an alternative until they switched to this online digital format that allowed them to scan it all in. Saved them the work of two people who could then concentrate on other things.

2. Create space. Allow them to give feedback on the story or encourage it by saying something like "Have you experienced anything like that?" Chances are they have and will be eager to tell you their story. That's when you know you have them. They can identify and have first hand pain points.

Take into consideration having to localize contracts according to regional laws. Digital communication around identifying information, privacy laws, taxation discrepancies etc. Consult with an attorney in the given region if need be, talk to internal CPA's or legal teams and make sure all of your ducks are in a row to avoid headache down the line.

Creating a partner workbook can be a useful tool. Here are some examples from one that Andrea created in a previous role.

Things we love about this

It educates partners on how to sell differently. Here partners had come from a hardware background and now wanted and needed to be able to sell software, but did not know how. They had the relationship with the right customers so were still valuable and highly influential.

The workbook provides a tool for Channel Managers to use to schedule meetings and an agenda to go through creating standardization across an organization.

There are tangible KPIs and measurable targets throughout including the partner scorecard which can be used to create competition among partners.

Managed Document Services Channel Partner Workbook

Planned Sales Activities

Partners who are successful generating incremental MDS opportunities do so with ongoing internal and external activities that keep Managed Document Services front of mind with sales teams and customers alike. There are many ways to get the message out and encourage customers to consider MDS.

Do you have specific offers within the MDS suite that you want to focus on this year?

Are there any obstacles to your promoting the whole product suite?

What 3 marketing activities can we commit to this quarter?

Suggestions:

- Direct mail campaign to existing and new customers. Have you seen our *cobranded templates?*
- Look at upcoming and current tenders and if MDS can be included.
- Internal sales training and incentive programs. *Are you aware of what is available?* Contact us if you are interested in launching something specific with your sales teams.
- Customer price promotion. Why not create *a special price bundle*. Ask us for advice on this.
- Customer event or hands-on workshop dedicated to Managed Document solutions. We would love to host your customers at our Innovation Centre or can bring our team to their office.

89

Managed Document Services Channel Partner Workbook

YOUR CHANNEL PARTNER SCORE CARD

We want our Partners to embrace this new portfolio and to be actively promoting and selling Manage Document Services.
Where are you on the MDS thermometer and how can we ensure progress is made every month?

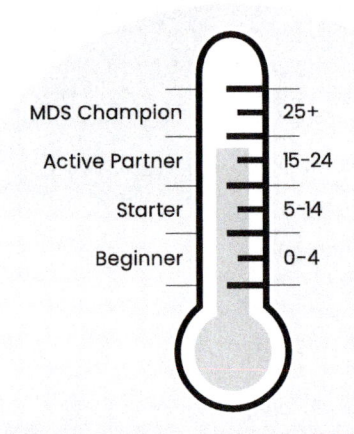

	MDS Thermometer
MDS Champion	25+
Active Partner	15-24
Starter	5-14
Beginner	0-4

Criteria	Enter Month
Sales & Technical Training	
Joint business planning	
Marketing activities	
Weekly pipeline updates	
Promote available incentives	
Adding MDS as value add to RFP's	
Attending webinars & deal clinics	
Conducting QBRs to promote innovation	
Hosting your own MDS event	
This month's score	

0 = nothing, 1 = poor, 2 = average, 4 = good, 5 = excellent

OUR STORY
Small Local Accounting Firm: approximately 30 employees and 20 freelances, 3 offices and remote working.

A local accounting firm has been successful over the past 5 years growing to have 3 offices with 5-10 people working in each as well as 20 freelancers who work from home.

Their clients are everything from one man trades people to larger businesses and they are growing.

Clients send in documents in numerous formats including a shoe box full of receipts from their plumber and builder clients. Everything comes into the main office who then have a small team that opens each one and then repackages to post to the relevant person's desk or office.

In addition to these, payments need to be made for taxes on behalf of some clients which requires the approval of both the client and someone internally at the firm.

The two main owners who sign off on everything are now increasingly busy travelling around to offices or out generating new business.

There are lots of statutory rules related to deleting information or having contracts resigned within a certain time that they find difficult to manage.

One person had a calendar with all this information on but recently when she was off sick it the whole process came to a standstill.

Their outbound mail has increased massively with the need to post reminders about tax assessment due dates or changes in government legislation. They have also developed a niche expertise around construction and have started marketing their services by sending out marketing material.

What is the cost of an inefficient process?

Cust. Order Bad Debt Report – Data Analysis			
Path Type	No. of Steps	Process Duration dd:	hh:mm:ss
Total steps	23	2	01:03:00
Typical path	14	2	00:27:00
Shortest path	10	0	00:46:00
Longest path	15	2	00:32:00

Printing and Paper			
Cust. Order Overpayments Report	No. of Steps	Process Duration dd:	hh:mm:ss
Printing	1	0	00:01:00
Handling	4	0	00:35:00

Cust. Order Overpayments Report			
Cost of Paper bourne content	Units	Unit Cost	Total Cost
Printing (Clicks and paper)	14	£0.020	£0.28
Handling time in minutes (Printing, annotating/filing/shredding)	35	£0.21	£7.35
		Total	£7.63

Printing and Handling		
Average cost per report	£4.62	
Total number of reports printed and handled	8	per day
	30	days
	£1,108	per month

Actioning Report Information		
Average cost per report	£12.50	
Number of reports actioned	8	per day
	30	days
	£3,000	per month

Total cost per month	**£4,108**
Cost per Annum	**£49,291.20**

Creating a partner journey map which you may or may not share with the partner can also be a useful tool both to keep track of what stage each partner is at as well as to explain your partner strategy and progress internally.

Partner Journey Map — OPENSPACE

Key Stages	Negotiating	Forming	Storming	Performing
Activities	Learning about product; Reviewing commercial agreement	Onboarding; Training; Create a marketing plan	Beginning to market technology; Generating initial leads	Generating ongoing leads; Closing buisness on a regular basis
Touchpoints	Understanding ideal partner persona	Partner prospecting and onboarding; Partner sales enablement; Kick of call - GTM strategy		Weekly pipeline support reviews; Monthly virtual meetings; Quaterly buisness review; Quaterly in-person meetings; Biannual inspirational podcast series; In-person visits; Events
Motivating Factors	Interest in technology; Opportunity to make money	Evidence of potential in product and technology; Guidance provided by marketing plan	Initial success from low - hanging fruit (easy sales)	Money made; Deals closed; Ongoing success
Key Partner Considerations	"Will the ROI be worth my time and effort?"; How soon will I get paid?; "Will this help us sell other products or services?"; What does commercial agreement look like?"; "Is the technology right for our market?"; "Can we sell this?"	"Do I understand the technology enough to sell it?"; "Do I feel confident in my ability to market this tecnology?"	"How do I reach better prospects?"	"How can I continue to build buisness?"; "What new technology has been introduced?"; "How do I stay informed?"
Partner Feelings	Intrigued; Excited	Hopeful, Potentially Overwhelmed	Overwhelmed (Highs and lows)	Self-sufficient, Motivated, Accomplished
Buisness Goals	Attract ideal partners	Onboard partners	Help partners close initial deals	Maintain successful partners
Partner Count		37	17	8
Opportunities	Improve partner outreach	Enhance GTM strategy	Reach out to partners with assistance; Improve partner resources	Meet with partners more often; Improve ongoing support; Host more partner events

Partner Return on Investment (PROI)

From the initial prospecting and negotiation to ongoing incentives and motivation woven throughout all the corporate lingo lies good old fashioned "what's in it for me".

Partners are run by people. Unusually relatively small operations owned by one person or a small group who are financially driven. They tend to fall into two categories. Either inventor or technician, or the sales person. If you have read books like Gerber's eMyth (recommend!) you will know that most small businesses fail because the baker who made pies for someone else suddenly decides to go it alone to have more freedom, control and money. They soon learn that rather than baking pies which is the bit they know and love, they are now having to do marketing, sales and accounting which they know nothing about and do not enjoy.

If you are standing in front of an entrepreneur that has been in business for some years they have against all odds, that now include a global pandemic, managed to overcome all that. Yet once you have tasted the fear of losing it all, not being able to pay workers or pay your kids school fees or your mortgage, you never really get over it. it is always in your mind somewhere. Many think or assume that channel partners are run by men with lots of greed and even bigger egos. What we see are families with the fear of failure.

There is no such thing as business. There are only people. When you are working with partners, what does that mean? Who are the people? What are they motivated by? When we meet partners for the first time we always ask "Is this your baby"? Followed by "well done." In those few words we bond. We tell them, without saying the words, that we know they struggled. We know how much they have invested and what this means to them and we are going to be gentle with that. We respect them because they are still here.

Give them the space to talk about their journey. Listen to how they started the business, the blood sweat and tears. Let them share what they are proud of. Listen to the business they lost and how they are rebuilding, struggling. Understand. Take the time to care. The stories are truly fascinating and have been highlights of our careers. These entrepreneurs are inspiring and so many have against all odds overcome so much uncontrollable adversity like wars, natural disasters and everything in between.

So yes "what's in it for them" is important and while some are thinking about funding their next designer watch or yacht, most are thinking about things far more basic, keeping going and keeping profitable.

> *Hint: Take a look at the section on who to hire. This is part of the reason why I love and highly value entrepreneurs. If you have tried to run your own business of any kind, whether you have succeeded or not, you have such intrinsic empathy for other entrepreneurs and channel partners are started, owned and led predominantly by entrepreneurs.*

It is so important to understand who you are working with before you try to convince them that selling your widget is going to be the best thing they ever did.

A useful tool is a partner Return on Investment (ROI) ROI calculator. These can be fancy physical pieces like the sort used for weight loss or in the building trade which are great for event giveaways or if you are doing a speed dating partner recruitment event. The takeaway then is quite literally a tool that shows them how much money they will make if they partner with you.

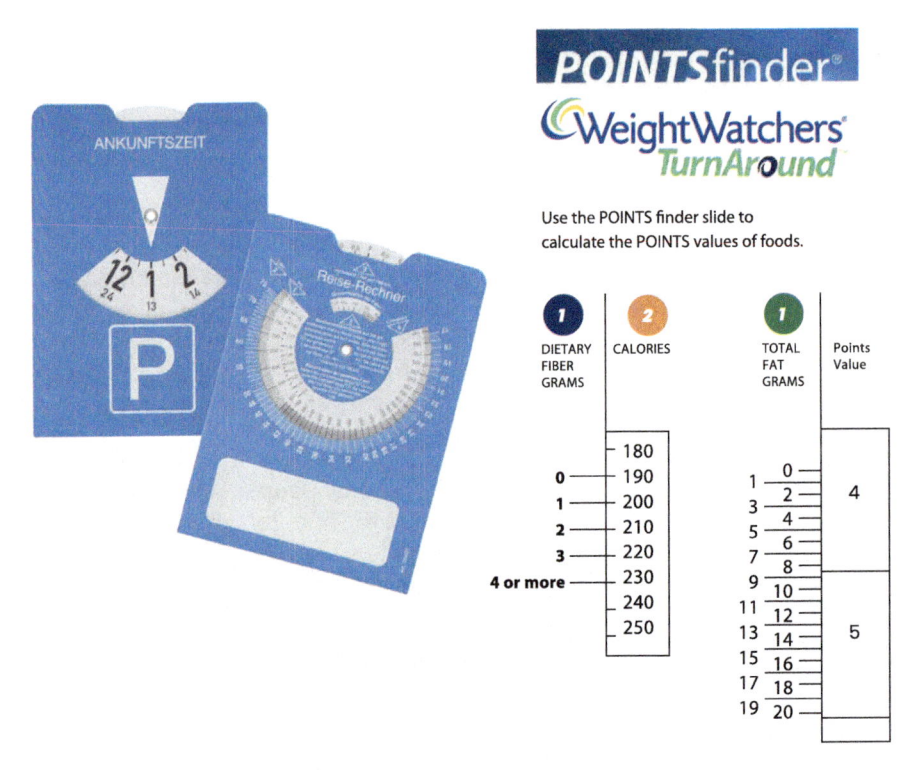

Partner calculators can also be simple using an excel spreadsheet. The fancy ones all start with that anyway. If you are a lowly channel manager working for a big organization and feeling a bit overwhelmed or lost, wondering how you are going to make an impact with the partner and stand out within the organization, this is a great place to start. It shows you have an intrinsic understanding of what you are selling and shows partners you are not afraid to cut to the chase and have a conversation about what you know matters to them.

Calculation considerations

As we have discussed in more detail elsewhere, partnerships often fall into two buckets; sales and service. It is easier if you split those two things out in any calculator even if you have a partner that is interested in both and add them together at the end.

94

Be honest about the success rate. Partners are not going to win every deal they submit a lead for.

Be realistic about the timeline. If you have a long sales cycle that will affect a partner's annual profitability with you or perhaps there is a ramp up period that you need to call out.

Keep in mind that what is important to one partner or in one business may be quite different in another scenario. Presenting a partner with a calculator that does not talk to what is important to them is like handing them a ticket on why not to work with you.

This my friends is why we started this section with the importance of understanding who the partner is and what is important to them. There is just no shortcut to that. This is the cornerstone of any channel professional. Leaders if you have an underperforming channel it is also worth going back to basics and digging into this to make sure nothing was missed. This is the absolute foundation of channel sales.

We find it useful to do this exercise with a what's in it for them ROI calculator whether you ultimately choose to share it with the partner or not. Here is a good example of that.

Example of an internal sales ROI Calculator

	PRODUCT 1	PRODUCT 2
Cost/Customer Price	$5,000	$10,000
Discount/Commission	20% of $1,000 = $200	20% of $2,000 = $400
Accessories	5% of $500 = $25	10% of $1000 = $100
Total Commission	$225	$500
Annual Lead Target	40	10
Average sales cycle	60 days	120 days
Estimated close rate H1	10% (4)	10% (4)
Estimated close rate H2	20% (8)	20% (1)
Annual	$2,700	$2,500
Estimated hourly rate	$15	$25 (you may need a senior sales engineer to help sell a more complicated product)
Estimated selling hours	16	32

	PRODUCT 1	PRODUCT 2
Total Procurement costs This could be more detailed to include others who touch the sales process for a more accurate cost.	$240	$800
Net profit per product	$2,460.00	$1,700

What does this highlight?

Although on the surface product 2 looks attractive it is more time consuming to sell and the ratio of success is lower making it less attractive.

"Where is their skin in the game" is what we hear all the time. It is common to want a partner to do some marketing to support the launch of your product locally. Before you ask them to do this take a look at this ROI.

If a partner is making $2,460 per annum, $205 per month how much of that should we reasonably expect them to invest themselves? The answer is zero. Really really zero. In fact so zero that this is not an attractive venture.

The calculator in the example has been conservative in terms of the number of people involved in the sales cycle.

This could include:

- Sales Manager
- Sales Engineer
- Customer success/Implementation
- Service and support
- Finance and accounting
- Operations

The more complicated the sale and sales cycle, the more people who are normally required on the partner side or for a small partner the more hours that one person will spend on this. If you have a complex sales cycle and low Annual Recurring Revenue (ARR) that is not going to be attractive. Also is it ARR for the partner? It often is for the manufacturer but partners are often seen as part of customer acquisition so that commission or discount is a one time thing and when the customer renews the partner gets zero. If you do offer commission in the second year this is known as annuity. The conversation about annuity starts right from the early prospecting and then contract negotiations.

Annuity is key because it affects how you view the initial discount or commission. If it is a one off customer acquisition fee your year two revenue will be +20% or more if you have expanded the relationship with the customer because they now love you and are selling more.

It is not common practice to do these ROI partner calculators and even less common to share them in this detail with the partner. The truth is that most partners do not consider the details of the procurement costs until they have had some experience and been through the process a few times. So you could just cross your fingers, hope they do not notice and hope for the best. Seriously! This happens all the time, so you could…HOWEVER that approach is not scalable! At some point our experienced entrepreneur wakes up and thinks "hang on a minute! This is taking up so much of our team's time that they cannot do and sell other stuff and I am only making $2K per year? Not worth it".

Now what happens next is interesting because although they think this they may or may not convey that concern to you. In our experience they usually do not. What happens instead is a deterioration in the relationship because they have decided to invest less and do less.

All of a sudden the partner hasn't completed their training or isn't running any events. On social media they seem to be promoting other stuff instead. Leads are down.

Lazy or if we are a bit more generous with our wording inexperienced channel managers may then campaign internally for an incentive because surely that would do the trick? If in doubt, throw money at the problem and the partner right? Well in the example of our ROI calculator how much do you think you would need to throw at that partner to get their attention and make a difference?

Here's our view:

1. Once you blow it and a partner decides this is not a profitable enough venture it is extremely difficult to win them back. There are so many other things they can sell and others will be knocking at their door. They are likely to have moved on long before you find out.
2. Throwing incentives to correct a problem because your initial sales proposition was ineffective is just not the way to go. It creates the wrong behavior. Partners can come to expect this and do nothing until they get it.
3. Bite the bullet. If you lose the partner, get into a fail fast mind set and reassess. This is where our next chapter comes in. What are you asking the partner to sell? Why are we allowing them to sell product 2 at all?

i. Perhaps we look for ways of reducing the partners product one procurement costs to make it more profitable?
ii. Perhaps we increase the partner margin from the get go.
iii. Perhaps we make this a referral partnership rather than a reseller in recognition that there simply is not enough in it for them.

Two other bits (that we couldn't think where to put so are just chucking in here 😄)

Partner enablement

How much training is involved and required in your onboarding? Partners will consider that in their own mental ROI calculator. You might want to as well. There will initially be a deficit in terms of the partner investments and reward. How long does it take them to recover that? This is why we promote shorter bite sized training that educates a partner gradually and regularly rather than long arduous and painful sessions that highlight how much time has been spent on your product and has them focus on how soon they are going to get pay back right from the start.

See the section on partner enablement where we unpack this a bit more.

Marketing

Similar to training. At your kick-off meeting did you convince or request the partner do some initial launch activities to promote the brand? Sounds sensible. Only now six months in when they are not making any money they remember that $1,000 spent on Google ads and the 5 days stood at a trade show.

We usually start our process with the PROI because it is just so crucial affecting:

- What you allow the partner to sell
- How much margin you can give away
- What and how much training do we need for partners
- How much partner marketing dop we need for new partners
- If a partner program is a viable option right now

We hope you can now see that if you get that wrong it is game over. Sometimes that just takes a while to reveal itself which is costly in every way.

Packaging your product for partners

Having a message that is right for direct sales teams is not always the same as having a message that works for channel partners.

You've got sales people and you are winning business. Aren't you good to go? Just duplicate that with partners? Absolutely not.

There are some important differences between your sales people and indirect channel sales.

You have likely hired and trained sales people who report to you and your team. They are accountable to you and highly motivated by the expectations in their contracts and the financial health of the business that pays their salaries. You also have the ability to monitor these individuals in myriad ways whether you are working remotely or in-office. You can for the most part control them.

Now when it comes to channel partners you have no control. You can ask, you can beg, you can scream when they do not get it right but you cannot control them. Partners are independent business partners with their own objectives, their own set of priorities and their own internal structures of influence. The best you can do is ask and convince. There is more trust involved. You will need to trust that your channel partners are acting on your behalf in the manner in which you have modeled and have track and measure systems in place to make sure that they are doing exactly what they say they are doing.

Vetting your partners is an important and involved step in this process. One of the things that facilitates trust is communication. We are not just talking about well…how you talk. This applies to your product and solution too. This applies to both B2B and B2C. The ability to have your message, your brand, your goals, your desired quantifiable outcomes be clear and concise is paramount.

AVOID THIS COMMON PITFALL

Quite often what we see are partners that have been given highly complicated sales propositions. A very complex pitch with unachievable metrics and unattainable prospects.

When you are trying to teach someone to do something, clear messaging is required. After all, you are essentially teaching them to sell like you. That's a challenge.

What you have to take into account is that channel partners often sell a whole portfolio of products and services. They will never be 100% focused on whatever your product or solution is. Even when they are successful with it there is always a tendency to look for other solutions, keeping an eye on the market and the lastest shiny shiny which allows them to go back to their customers with something new.

Businesses often obsess about having partners be exclusively committed to them. Partners are always reluctant to do this because they do not want to put all their eggs in your basket. If they do agree they have likely held you to ransom for it with extortionate commission or discount rates. Rather than trying to find exclusivity, make yourself unforgettable. Keeping channel partners active, motivated and engaged is doable. Think of entertaining a child: keep it interesting, keep it simple. Create a simple value proposition with a simple workflow and process that's achievable and saleable.

There is an assumption that you can just take exactly what you have done with your direct sales team, package that up with a different color bow and deliver it to your indirect sales team. This just does not work. You do not completely have to recreate the wheel and of course you can leverage content, tools and methodologies you use with the direct team.

Let us look at some examples:

- ABC Company has a software solution.
- There is a base model, a financial vertical, and let us say several modules one can add on.
- Sufficient R and D has been done on Modules A, B and C but Module D is still in beta testing.

The company is confident it is going to be a lucrative and well-performing facet of the product but it has had a couple of challenges. The director, having access to all of that information, has released the solution to the direct sales team to sell. She is confident her sales people can still speak to the advantages of Module D because they have access to a sales engineer who's going to guide them and can list limitations and caveats around how and where it is sold. Perfectly reasonable and a common event in sales particularly for businesses in hyper growth mode where they cannot afford to standstill and are constantly juggling development and selling.

This same set of circumstances in the hands of a channel partner could have catastrophic results. First of all, sales people have, for the most part, happy ears, so they are going to take in all of the information, ignore half the caveats that you have given them and they are going to say whatever they need to say to get the product sold. This could result in somebody having a solution that is not right for them or bring something prematurely to a market. Thus leading to poor publicity, negative brand associations, loss of clientele, the list goes on.

Here's what we would recommend instead: you take what you have got for the direct team but instead of allowing the indirect team access to the whole line we scale that back and we just allow them to put the core product forward. Then a phased approach. Maybe taking one or two trusted partners and slowly working on a roll out or an expansion of what you allow the channel to sell in a more controlled environment. That way we are constantly monitoring, measuring, and testing the partner's ability to sell and to articulate potential problems. As a result, we may need some more sales enablement or training, we may need to look back at how we remunerate the partner or what we say to them contractually, for example.

Another area that you need to consider when you are assessing if channel is right for you is whether or not your product or solution is productized. You have to be able to package it up to enable somebody else to sell it on your behalf.

Even if you are not an e-commerce solution, think about your productization that way. If you had to create a digital store, where prospective clients could make informed decisions about your products, add them to a cart, purchase and have their items arrive swiftly and correctly, could you?

Whether you are an e-commerce solution or not, that's the level of simplicity you need to be working with.

Here's an example:

- Company EFG sells a product that's in a box. But when the sales team brings the box to market it has 23 SKU's of different parts and bits and associated software that needs assembly and who knows what else. That is not something that is ready and ripe for the channel. You cannot dump that on to Channel partners. If you cannot take what your internal sales team are doing (who, by the way, would also appreciate a more sellable product) and refine it to a point of reasonable simplicity, channel is not for you.
- Looking at the same problem through another lens, an asset you have to delicately account for is time. Every stakeholder in this endeavor enters with their best interest in mind, partners included. These stakeholders are discussing the time investment they have made in order to sell your product, and what ROI they are seeing on that time invested.

Another example:

- Company XYZ has an incredible product with a 6-month sales cycle.
- If your partner is getting 10% and the minimum sales value was $5,000 (and quite often even large Enterprise customers would start with the $5,000 solution) you have got somebody who has done phone calls and meetings and emails backwards and forwards for a 6 month sales cycle only to be getting $500.
- Having a productized solution or service requires a reasonable sales cycle.

How much are they willing to do for that? How much would you be willing to do it for?

If you are not able to answer these questions, if you are curious how your brand will be received in the marketplace or unsure if you have got a sellable product in its purest form: here's another indication that you need to step back and do some research. Have a qualified market research firm field a study and gather that crucial data. High quality, data-driven insights are the key to answering these questions succinctly and exactly what is needed before you are able to move forward with a partner portal.

Productizing for Channel

Nine times out of ten, when we get questions about whether or not a solution is developed enough or solid enough for someone to sell on their behalf, it is not a matter of development. On the contrary, it is more often than not about massively simplifying. Stripping away layers that were in place because they had the luxury of coordinating with their internal sales team. A team you can dictate to, manage and control and who have been fully involved in and solely dedicated to the sales of this product/solution are far more able to digest that complex picture. With indirect sales teams, you just do not have that mindshare. it is not about what you need to do in terms of content creation or additional development. That might look like paring down to your core offering. This doesn't mean you won't be able to sell more complex solutions either now or in the future with your direct sales team. With the channel team, however, at least in the beginning and perhaps through the entirety of your relationship with them, you keep it simple. Limit what you market through channel partners.

Ideally, channel partners are able to process quickly - not to be burdened with managing anything that's overly complicated. They need access to the right experts and the sales engineers should issues come up. They want to be given a couple of choices. If you think about this in the SKU world, if you have got a software offering package with twelve items and one standard hardware item: consider limiting marketing the hardware item through channel partners. Think about how that could streamline logistics for the partner portal: you can now figure out a median shipping price for that item for any country.

Think of it more as a strategic, intentional, land and expand: get your partner to get that new logo, get that new piece of business, get them up and running. Then have your customer success team expand. You might think "well, I could have the channel partner do that from the get-go." Sure. But it will lengthen your sales cycle and your lead will be sitting with your channel partner, not with you. What you want to do is get that lead in, activated and happy - using your solution. Then grow that relationship with them.

Getting it right the first time

It may seem tempting to do just the opposite: find a channel partner, give them a half-baked version of your product in the name of testing the waters or not giving away too many trade secrets. you are in growth mode, your direct sales team is fairly sorted and you are eager to expand to the rest of the world.

Instead, pause, rewind and take a look at where you really are in the process. If we are all honest with each other we know it is a process of evolution. We know the product is going to go through several iterations. Frankly it is important that it does. That we are dynamic and adaptable. But when presenting to a channel partner, there are some big No's.

Do not experiment with your product with a channel partner. As previously mentioned, it is OK if you have additional modules yet to come on a piece of software or a platform. it is OK if you foresee further iterations of the product you currently have on the market. However, channel partners should receive products and solutions that have been fully baked and successful in the marketplace. They are about to invest their resources to promote you and they do not want to do that for something that is not fully baked. It is a small world. You will burn bridges and you are unlikely to recover from that.

Think about how diverse your portfolio is. How many variations, versions, expansions, etc. of your product there are? Limit them to one or two. Then go even further and simplify the business process behind that product line. How do partners get the price? How do they process the sale? The whole workflow needs to be streamlined. If you make it too arduous to do, they quite simply won't do it.

A note on pricing: People often fail to think about pricing in different markets. You have most likely created your pricing model in your home country. In order to thoroughly understand what that pricing should be in other countries research is required. We cover more on the importance of research in Part 3.

- Have qualified researchers take a look at the market you are going into - who are the competitors?
- Who are the alternative sources? What's the average salary of the average person in your target market?
- Do you have boots on the ground in your target market to assess the opportunities and the potential challenges?

Perhaps, for example, you have a platform that requires internet access. If you have coordinated your pricing in the developed world where, for the most part, the internet is free and easily accessible, you may run into problems in parts of Africa where they do not have that luxury. Making constant changes will result in setting your channel partner up for failure and frustration as they try to adjust mid-pitch. This can be avoided by partnering with a research firm that has global reach and experience in the vertical that you are in.

Deciding whether channel is for you depends on your current internal team. While channel partners are an outsourced solution to an internal goal, they need to be managed. Think about how you would train your direct sales team to provide sales enablement for your indirect team. More on managing channel partners later in this book.

If you have not thought thoroughly about your contract (is it localized to your target market, have you thought about local currency or local data protection statutes?) you are not prepared for channel.

Finally, do you have the time and the bandwidth to take this on? As a business leader or decision maker, it is important to assess whether you have enough time, energy or a deep enough bench to delegate these processes. To create any partner program takes 3 to 6 months of strategizing. Any additional time is around bureaucracy and internal stakeholders and lack of approval or lack of budget to get things done.

Ok. So you have done the work to truly assess whether channel is right for you and you have decided it is. Congratulations! Now what? Don't worry, we've got you covered. The following chapters will delve into just how to prepare, plan, productize, price and stack your team to best support your channel partner. And what to do if, despite your best efforts, it has gone up in flames.

Ditch the Fluff. Make Channel Measurable.

One of the common accusations or silent criticisms of channel as a department within an organization is that channel is seen as a bit fuzzy and lacking in the solid tangible metrics of direct sales. There is no real reason for that. It is certainly possible to have KPIs and metrics. This often unspoken perception will affect everything from if you get promoted to whether you get budget allocation.

It is often easier for us to see things in others than in ourselves.

When we meet with channel partners they often have very ambiguous actions and goals. Part of the work we do with partners and with organizations is setting up the structure that turns these into measurable goals. it is all related and connected. You have a strategy with measurable metrics and that should feed down into the targets you give your partners and how you intend to manage and measure them.

Initial kick off meeting and Quarterly Business Reviews (QBRs)

This sets the stage for how things will work moving forward. Part get to know you and part establish the expectations. This should be no surprise to anyone and a seamless continuation of what was agreed during negotiations and the contract.

Channel managers can come unglued here if they have fudged the negotiations saying yes to everything or being vague about the expectation in order to get an attractive partner to say yes and sign up. It is then impossible to rock up to the first meeting and start outlining expectations that were never discussed, the partner was not aware of and doesn't like. The result is that you have a partner who looks good on paper and in theory but has not been set up for success and may not be right for you. Or you may not be right for them.

Often we have been brought in to organizations to clean up some sort of channel mess. Discovering this is so common. Or perhaps you are a channel manager that has inherited a channel and suddenly discovers you have the wild wild west of channel partners doing whatever they want with little structure because things were not set up correctly from the get go.

Are you with us so far? Consistency is key.

1. What you say during negotiations should reflect what you say in the contract. Do not try to sneak things you know will be unpopular that you are too chicken to say to the partner in the contract. Call it out. If it's a no, it's a no. Be honest. Always.
2. What you say in the contract should reflect what you say in the kick off meeting. The actions and activities agreed should be specific, documented,

shared and agreed. You establish regular quarterly business review (QBRs) to check in and assess.

3. What you say in your QBRs should reflect what you agreed during the kick off and the expectation set in the contract. No one should be surprised here!

This approach empowers you to say things like:

Let us talk about the leads. We agreed that you would generate 50 per quarter. You shared that you would do two in person events and one webinar as lead generation activity. I see that you did not do those events and you have not generated any leads this quarter. I am disappointed by that. Please can you help me understand what is going on.

> Tip: You should NEVER wait until the end of a quarter if you know something is wrong and you should know something is wrong every day and week when those leads do not come in and those events do not happen.

This QBR template can also be used for your initial kick off meeting.

Managing multiple partners and keeping track of progress

We love a heat map! Heat maps come in all different formats but essentially it is a traffic light system:

Red: Nothing has happened

Amber: Something has happened

Green: Everything you want to happen has happened!

You can use whatever colors you want and are not restricted to only three. Create a key that works for you and what you want to show. As a leader what I am expecting to see is that on day one there was lots of red and by day 91 there was way more green.

> Tip: Do not make your heat map overly complicated. It is supposed to tell a story at a glance.

This is the sort of heatmap used in direct sales or where you are monitoring pipeline and leads on a more granular level. An alternative is generating reports using software like SalesForce and Tableau. A lot depends on how you like the information presented. I often find that the process of updating the heatmap is useful and like the quick look it provides.

This is a typical partner heat map. You can immediately see that all partners are through the initial onboarding stage. The "listed" column refers to being listed on the manufacturer website which could require an additional action from the partner or is perhaps something waiting for an internal department to action.

Heat maps can be done for all your partners or split by region or product group. Find what works for you. We suggest a different tap for each quarter so you can show that progression (or not!).

Senior leadership does not usually have time to get into the weeds so showing two heat maps from the previous and current quarter, one with lots of red and the other with lots of green shows progress and that you are on top of things.

If you are managing a lot of partners it is difficult to keep track and remember who's who and who's done what. Heat maps are a great tool for your own internal time management and prioritizing. it is easy to have all your time sucked away by the more active partners and then miss that there are partners you should be nurturing.

With large channel partners the relationships can be complex. It is important to have a plan for how you intend to manage the account. Account planning, again so commonplace in direct sales but often non-existent with indirect channel sales is key. You cannot just drift along crossing your fingers and hoping for the best. Do your homework!

Who is this partner? Where have they seen success?

What is important to them?

Who do you know and are in contact with today?

Who should you know and have a relationship? What is your plan to get in front of them?

What are the strengths and weaknesses of the partner?

What are some of the risk factors to your relationship?

Where do you need internal support or think an executive connection would be valuable, like connecting your CEO to the partners CEO for lunch or a chat.

Account plans, like heat maps, can and should show progression over time. They should not be stagnant.

By having the QBRs and heat maps Channel Managers are able to track against agreed actions.

Sometimes it is useful to think backwards. What do you want your outcome objective to be? At the end of it all, what metrics do you want to be able to showcase? From that you can then think about what data you need to capture in order to generate that sort of report.

If you are working with a CRM like SalesForce.com you should integrate that into your channel process. This can be expensive.

Realistic first year expectations

It is very difficult to use any first year wins as indicative of what your program will look like and what you will achieve in the future. Within the first 12 to 18 months, particularly if you are building a channel program from scratch, you will learn so much, make some mistakes and incorrect assumptions.

You are building a whole new set of business processes and practices.

You are building a new system, gathering internal mindshare.

You are empowering your teams internally to understand what their part in the program is.

You are figuring out who partners should be and how best to work with them.

For the partners you are setting expectations, teaching them about your product or solution. It is tempting to set sales targets, and if it makes you more productive or serves as a motivational tool for you and your team, set them. But (perhaps only in your mind) expect not to hit them.

The initial revenue you might generate is that low-hanging fruit and is not indicative of the program or success you may have going forward. Once you have moved on from calling in all of your favors, through your low-hanging fruit to a trickle of qualified leads, to a steady stream of qualified leads and a consistent conversion rate, then you can start managing revenue expectations.

Let us look at an example:

Example

We created a Channel program that launched in March 2021 and it is now December 23rd December 2021. During that time frame we achieved the following:

- Pipeline - $3.3 million
- Closed opportunities 25, valued of $356,000
- Average sales price of $1,000
- Conversion rate of 10%
- Compared to with marketing leads a conversion of 5%

What we can see is good quality leads that have a high propensity to convert to sales. They have a higher propensity to close than marketing leads do and when they close they are closing at a higher average sales price.

We also track the time it takes to complete a channel sale.

Average Channel sales cycle: 36 Days

Average Direct sales cycle 52 Days

In our experience it takes 2-3 years of collecting and analyzing this sort of data to properly be able to predict and efficiently forecast.

Leadership: Challenge your Channel Teams

Like anyone else and any other department, channel sales needs to be held accountable and challenged in order to reach their full potential. Channel is sometimes this big mysterious unknown.

As a result we often see that if senior leadership has limited experience with channel there is a reluctance to challenge that team the way a direct sales team might be. We get it. You do not know enough to have an informed and educated discussion. We hope this book will also empower leaders to ask more. Challenge more. Ultimately get more out of channel teams.

Here are a few questions you can ask that start to reveal potential pitfalls and identify if there is a real plan or if there is a lot of fluff.

Leadership Question: What results are you hoping to generate from that activity?

What you want to see: Specific metrics associated with actions

Not just a long term goal but what is the "sales cookbook"? What are the short term ingredients that go into achieving that? What do they expect to see every week, month and quarter in order to achieve that goal? This then gives you the data you need to track and question progress in real time rather than waiting till half way through the year to suddenly be reviewing the data and thinking "we are not going to make it". For sales leaders this is nothing new. You hold direct sales teams accountable in this way. For some reason channel teams have often got a free pass. That's a mistake.

Leadership Question: Please can I have a profile update of our top 10% of partners.

What you want to see: Each week get an introduction to one or two partners.

You are looking for a detailed partner account plan.

You want to see that the channel team understands everything about the partner and is actively building and expanding the relationship with them.

Who are the people? What else do they sell? Who do they sell to? Where have they been successful?

What is the deal we have with them? Commission structure? Any contractual nuances? Targets?

What have they achieved with us so far? Leads, sales or any other less tangible contributions like being an evangelist on social media.

What is the structure of their operation? What are their goals and aspirations? Is the owner looking to retire in two years with a yacht or has he just started his own business after a break up with a business partner that is the main competition? How do they generate leads? How are sales conducted? What's the process? Who are the sales people? Do they have dedicated marketing? What is their support structure? What is the culture? You want to get an idea of the culture and personality of the partner.

Leadership Question: What are our touch points with them?

What you want to see: A regular cadence of connections. In person, virtual, written. How are the channel team staying connected with them and front of mind?

Leadership Question: How have we grown (or plan to grow) the relationship?

What you want to see: Progress and a continuous plan to level up.

A better understanding of the partner. A better relationship with them.

More members of their team trained to represent your product or solution.

More marketing. More social media. More events.

More leads. More sales.

Partner Relationship Manager (PRM)

This is a software specifically designed to support partners and channel managers. What one does can be quite different to what another does and there is no point paying for functionality you will never use. It is important however to think ahead of what you may not need now but will grow into. PRM's create stickiness by integrating with your various business systems and becoming so intrinsic to the way that you do business it becomes very difficult to swap one out for another.

Start a spreadsheet and use some of the ideas and questions we have provided below as well as things that are important to your partners and internal teams. Examples like:

Do you want partners to be able to cobrand marketing materials themselves using the PRM?

Do you want partners to be able to see how much commission they have made and is in their pipeline?

Do you want pipeline updates partners make to instantly populate into fields within your CRM?

Any of these things can qualify in or out a PRM vendor.

There are lots of choices out there from the simple to the complex and fully integrated. Things to consider:

Some have their own CRM and some integrate with others

Some require a designer or developer skill set while others are built for you to be able to manage yourself.

Make sure you request a proof of concept

Ask the vendor to do a presentation to your entire team including finance, operations, sales enablement and marketing.

Questions to consider

- There are lots of nice features that can draw you in. They will often cost extra, like newsletter or social media features and may be the differentiator between one solution and another. How often will you use that feature? If you created an editable PDF template for your newsletter would that work and how much would you save?
- How technical and long is the training? Do you need and have someone inside your organization to manage that ?

- What does support look like and what are their SLA's?
- What is their ability to support other languages both the software and their services and what does that look like?
- What is their ability to handle multi currency?
- Do they have a partner enablement training module?
- Do they integrate with other softwares you use like Tableau for reporting for example

> Tip: Are you thinking of creating your own inhouse PRM? Don't bother. Seriously we have never ever EVER seen that end well. There is a reason specialist PRM software exists and why most with even a basic partner program will use one.

A lot of time we are swayed or drawn in by how pretty the UI looks. Literally the pretty pictures. Wait…is that just us Belinda?! Anyway, don't do that! Really try and focus on the functionality, what sort of process you can build out and what your ability to customize is and make it work for you. The pretty pictures are usually the easiest bit and have more to do with your own creativity. Even creating a custom landing page is rarely an issue whereas trying to solve for something that does not integrate or show partners the information they need to sell will be a deal breaker.

No paid for promotion here we promise! The choice of PRMs out there grows all the time so do your research. Here are three we like:

Impartner

Great tool and the basics are quite DIY

Spent approx $100,000 on essential customisations and integration work with SalesForce.com

U.K Sales knowledgeable and super helpful. Most of the support was based in the U.S and was a let down. Long delays to get answers and get problems solved.

Allbound

Lots of good functionality.

In our instance the team needed a months of lead time to implement, so plan ahead or this will not be an option for you. You've got to respect a team that does not promise what they cannot deliver.

SalesForce.Com

This was the most expensive of the PRMs each time we have gone shopping BUT the cost of integrating others with SFDC costs you a pretty penny so you save there and the functionality is really seamless. If you have the budget and SFDC is your CRM we would be very tempted to go for this.

Please do not limit your search and assessment to these three. I would look at as many as you can. There will always be new vendors with creative approaches and maybe even developers who worked for one of the above who move on and come up with something even better under a different brand name. Have an open mind.

> *Tip: Many claim to be DIY but are actually not requiring so much of your time to learn how to manage it that it becomes impractical.*

Make friends with Finance!

Managing a channel partner program requires expertise in multidisciplinary, cross-functional team management. It often requires the spirit of the freelancer - a jack-of-all-trades disposition. Unlike direct and indirect sales teams, accounting departments typically lack a degree of urgency when it comes to the channel. Internal teams like finance and accounting need to come along on the journey with you and not have urgent channel requests dumped at their doorstep.

We discuss in the onboarding chapter more on interdepartmental collaboration but we want to specifically call out finance. Why? This is how your partners get paid and that my friends affects everything.

True story

Channel program launched

Channel partners onboarded

Leads coming in, sales being made

Marketing supporting, social media high fiving

It took this organization 6 months to pay the first partner who made a sale

That is a disaster!

- You are treading water, apologizing and getting frustrated for the entire 6 (ok maybe 5) months
- Finance is beyond annoyed at you and you are venting to your friends and family that surely anyone could simply get these people paid. You don't understand each other's world.
- Not paying your partners is commercial suicide. They (like most of us when we are honest) are primarily motivated by their compensation.
- Your partners are annoyed but more than that they immediately think three things:
    a. Is this really a company that I want to work with?
    b. I really need the money and have financial things based on this commission. If I cannot rely on them to pay me should I be doing this at all?
    c. If they are this inefficient at working with me as a partner can I really trust them with my precious customers that I have been nurturing and safeguarding for years. Their inability to handle billing makes us look incompetent and could jeopardize agreements for future selling opportunities.

It is very, very difficult to keep the partner and then not have that experience affect the rest of the relationship. In one way or another if they do stay they have an attitude of "you owe us" and "you are lucky we stuck around".

> Tip: The more bullish you become with finance and the more screaming and throwing your hands up in the air you do the longer this will take to fix. There is no shortcut and if you have totally neglected to bring them along on the journey, listen to their concerns and build a program around what they can deliver and when they can deliver it then that is YOUR problem to fix not theirs.

There is a need for internal education or departmental onboarding as well as the external work with partners. At the very least, a clear communication of expectations when it comes to channel work. We hope the following serves as a guide for how to properly work with your finance teams for seamless integration of a channel program and helps you to avoid some of the pitfalls.

1. Map out the channel program workflow. Finance does not need all the details. They are listening for where they come in and what will be asked of them.

2. Start collaborating early from the conception of the program. We recommend involving finance before you have engaged with legal to create your contract. How you pay partners, the targets they have, how these are measured and the timeline you commit to pay partners in, will all involve the finance team.

3. Multiple check ins are best. After you have their initial feedback and you go off and build the program, come back and check in with them again sharing the latest iteration. Double checking and giving them the opportunity to say "I didn't realize it would be like that. That won't work".

4. Summarize your meetings in short emails with bullet points of what you have agreed. They cannot start throwing their arms up at you if you have done all you can to consider and involve them. Copy in heads of department ending with a line "Please let me know if I have missed anything we should be considering".

5. When you start building something like the PRM or integration with the CRM or a partner invoice template - run this by finance. I know it is so tempting to live off email but if possible we would recommend grouping a few things you need their comment on and having a call. Not only does this help you build the relationship with those colleagues but it also helps you to get more detailed and direct feedback that people often hold back on putting in writing.

6. If you are doing any version of a trial run, having a pilot program or proof of concept for example, make sure the finance team is invited to these demonstrations and that you seek their input.

7. Document your workflow with a map showing the expectations you have of the finance team clearly. For example: Finance will pay partners within 30 days of close of sale confirmed upon receipt of signed contract. Run this by

the finance team in advance to get their input before launching. Quite often we see finance are told what is going to happen which gets their back up. Involving, consulting, speaking, collaborating. This is the way to go.

8. Be grateful. Your partner experience is linked heavily to your collaboration with finance. When that big sale comes in or your are getting that kudos please do not forget to thank your colleagues in finance who usually remain unseen in that crucial back of office process.

How to fix things

OK so you did not get this book in advance and you are picking this up when things have already gone pear shaped. How do you recover?

1. Apologize. Most issues occur not because of the initial problem but because of what we do next. Get a meeting (not email) and be honest. You messed up. You did not involve them at all or as much as you should and now it is a disaster.
2. Explain what you need emergency help with and that you take full responsibility for it and would appreciate anything they can do to support you.
3. Start again. You need to commit to doing all the work articulated above. Go through the program with them and be willing to acknowledge things they would want to see, changes that need to be made even if that is now expensive and inconvenient.

Things finance commonly misunderstands

Finance, often because of the way things work in the accounting world, regard and treat partners as vendors. Where you may get away with not paying that vendor that you buy a lot of office furniture from (also not nice) partners will not put up with this.

Finance often does not understand the nuances of the partner relationship.

True story

Meet the characters in our story:

A Distributor getting 40% commission

A reseller that works through him getting 20% commission

A sales person that works for the distributor getting 10% commission

Two other resellers, one getting 20% commission and another getting 10%

The mistake

Finance sends a report to all the characters. This report shows the company name and the level of commission they get.

To be efficient they attach a spreadsheet of all the partners contact details and ask them to verify so they can pay them as quickly as possible.

The drama

The commission level of each partner is confidential. The Distributor on 40% immediately has to deal with:

- Angry resellers in his downstream wanting to know why he gets 40% and gives so much less to them?
- Why do they only get 10% but another reseller gets 20%?
- The sales person who feels they did all the work is now insulted that everyone gets paid more than them.
- The Distributor is furious at the vendor that things held privately have now been disclosed
- Finance only produced a report based on fields of data extracted from the PRM and CRM. They cannot see what all the fuss is about. Well, they can by now but certainly did not have any concept of the ramifications when they sent it out.

In this story finance was very much still treating partners like vendors rather than people we want to thank for generously passing business our way. With vendors, you do not need to be as sensitive to how you make them feel. You have done them a favor buying their stuff and you can just send them any old email instructions on how they will be paid. With partners we care about the partnership experience and how we make them feel. Always. We are or should be, constantly thinking if we are treating them well. Fostering their trust and by proxy the trust of their customers (who we ultimately want to be our customers) will ensure they send us more business and do not ditch us for a competitor.

Another consideration here is that the information finance sent contained every partner's contact details, details of the sale and end user and drum roll... details of the commission each partner is paid. Why is this a problem? It is against every data protection legislation, particularly GDPR in Europe and UKI. The penalty for this are fines that go into millions of dollars. This also affects your brand reputation and can even affect your ability to get certain product certifications that require high standards of data protection. Partners often get different commissions as part of the negotiation process. Showing one partner is actually receiving more than another leads to general disharmony. Transparency is an important facet of corporate communication, but I am sure we can all agree certain information is intended for certain audiences, and not others.

Contractually you are likely to be in breach of your own partner agreement, most of which include language around a commitment to pay partners within a certain time frame. 30 days is good. 3 months is the maximum you can push that too. Remember every time you pay a partner they are motivated to sell more.

This type of mistake chips away at trust, the cornerstone of all good relationships. Partners get nervous about not only introducing their large enterprise customers to you but also impedes their ability to add additional resellers to sell your solution with all these mistakes and poor experience.

The bottom line is this: These blunders garner a negative effect on your channel growth and expansion that you may never recover from.

Summary

- Talk to each other. Have meetings to share concepts with finance and get feedback from the start
- Map out the process identifying any incorrect assumptions or problems
- Create a guide for partners complete with screenshots and instructions, run this by finance for approval

Cross Cultural Communication

The world is increasingly becoming a smaller and more multicultural place. Israel, Eastern Europe and India are currently killing it in terms of really innovative software development. Something that used to seem the exclusive home of silicon valley. When we ignore local differences and try to chuck a program over to other countries that has worked in our own there are a multitude of mistakes that get made.

Some of these are really subtle nuances but can come across as rude, insensitive and insulting. Hardly what we want when we are trying to get partners to engage and do business with us. If you are a Direct Sales Manager you will likely have a territory or vertical market and become expert in that. Quite often a Direct Sales person will be from and or live in the region they are selling into. They may also speak the language.

The same is not always true with Channel Managers. As a Channel Manager you usually have a much more expansive geographical area of responsibility. With that comes a responsibility to work with people across different countries and cultures in a way that at the very least does not cause offense. You may or may not have had direct experience of the countries you are responsible for. We have certainly met channel managers with international remits who don't own a passport.

Others have written more extensively on this topic and of course much can be achieved by taking the time to research the country and region you are going to and asking about things you are not sure about.

Here is an example using time zones. With some simple considerations and small changes you can show you have respect for your local partners. This enables you to connect better and positively reflects on the brand in general. We frequently see things like this that with a little forethought can be easily avoided.

Dealing with time zones

Do not send emails saying "can you make 2pm EST" because you can't be bothered to figure out what the local equivalent is. Work out what time that is in Jeddah, Lisbon or Liverpool. Set up different clocks in your calendar so you know what time it is there and do not have to ask or guess. There are lots of online tools and software to support this.

Be prepared to stay up late or get up early. Do not blindly expect partners to do that by sending meetings invites that are 4am their time. You should shoulder any inconvenience until you get a local partner manager.

Energy. Be your best self. Do not give them the sleepy or exhausted version of you and your team at every meeting just because they are in a different time zone.

Be conscious of cultural and religious differences that may affect time. For example: although Dubai changed its working hours to be more in line with the West making Saturday and Sunday weekends so that weekdays started on Monday instead of Tuesday, not all of the UAE has adopted this. Even if they have in theory in practice most of the Middle East closes at noon on a Friday for prayers and works on a Sunday. Know that and do not send emails on a Friday afternoon out of respect if you do not have to.

You could argue that they will get to it when they are back in office and we know many of muslim partners that would support that. However, if nothing we are sending on a Friday afternoon is an emergency, out of respect, we hold off. Similarly, even if it is light touch, keep an eye on emails on a Sunday. Remember that it is their Monday and they are ready to get selling. You wouldn't want to miss an opportunity nor show any disrespect.

Quite often channel teams have led an organization in its understanding of the global landscape and development as a true global organization.

- Look for opportunities to introduce your local partners to other departments within the business. This helps educate them as well as promoting your channel program.
- Share your findings about how things are done in other regions and the differences you have identified. This can help everything from the development of future sales strategies to product roadmaps.

Partner Marketing

Partner marketing is marketing specifically designed for partners. This could mean a campaign to attract and recruit new partners as well as marketing that we want the partner to use to target the end customer they are reselling to.

People with specific partner marketeer experience are quite limited and those who can demonstrate real tangible past success are even more scarce. This specialist role tends to be the luxury of big brands and with that come some challenges. If you are hiring someone that has only ever worked for a big brand with deep pockets and lots of resources they will have ideas about partner marketing based on that. They may not be as effective at developing and launching a program for a startup without all that.

Similarly big brands tend to work with larger, more sophisticated and well established resellers. The persona of these partners, as we have discussed earlier, is completely different to your mom and pop small reseller or independent consultant.

We do not think you necessarily need someone who is specialist in partner marketing as long as you have a mature channel team who knows what they are doing and what they want to achieve. We have had a great deal of success working with a general marketing department or even an external agency to leverage what we have rather than recreate the wheel, for channel partners.

> *Tip: This is very much personal preference but in our experience ideas and energy start to get a bit stale after a while working with the same marketing team. You can get so much out of a new person joining the team, using freelancers instead or asking for a different member of the team to lead. Just changing the designer can achieve this however if the marketing brief is written by the same marketing person that may start to lack luster and the designer will only be as good as the direction they are given.*

There are some key things to be aware of and you may need to help educate the marketing team if they are not familiar with the way your channel partner program works.

1. **Sellers.** In the channel we sell twice. We sell a concept to the channel partner and get them to sell that to the end user. If you use a Distributor there are three sales and adding a Global Systems Integrator possibly gives you 3 or even 4 players selling as part of the sales cycle. Understanding who any marketing piece will be targeting and who will be using it is key. A good partner marketing program will acknowledge and speak to each one of the sellers and influencers.

2. **Timeline**. When working with partners we are asking them to communicate something out to another audience. As a result a Reseller will have a calendar of their own marketing activities and a budget. A Distributor will

not bombard their resellers everyday but also have their own calendar of those activities. Partners plan in advance to encompass all the messages they want to get out. Seasonality and holidays also affect when messaging can go out. Channel Managers need to be sensitive to this and plan ahead so that your partners can also plan ahead. This means they need information in advance if you want campaigns to run at the same time as the direct team. We would recommend 6-9 months advance planning.

    a. **9 Months** - Provide partners with a brief outline of dates for campaign releases and what will be expected of them.

    b. **6 Months** - Provide partners with more detail about what each of the campaigns will include with a more detailed explanation of the contents, deliverables and expectations.

    c. **3 Months** - Present partners with everything they need to be successful with the campaign. This should include templates, battle cards, creative, co branded materials, incentives, bundled promotions and training on anything new.

3. **Listen.** Local partners have experience with what works and what does not in their regions. Use this to help inform your partner marketing efforts.

Example: Paper vs. digital. In the western world, it is easy for us to believe print is dead, digital is king and a lack of an online presence for a company is a red flag. However, in many parts of the world, print marketing is not only hugely successful, but it is still considered the gold standard. This is still the case even if those countries have the infrastructure for digital marketing to be successful. As we mentioned earlier in parts of the Middle East and Africa, for instance, the thickness of your business card still matters. Being in print is still hierarchically considered to be important. Therefore having print advertising while almost non existent in one region might be really important in another.

Proactive vs. reactive partner marketing

For partner marketing there tend to be two camps. Proactive Partner Marketing and Reactive Partner Marketing. Reactive partner marketing relies on the partner coming to you with their needs:

Do you have a brochure about this?

Can we have something that is co-branded?

We are appearing at this tradeshow. Could you please help us fund it?

We need this in an additional language, can you provide that?

We want to create a bundle offer with your solution and another. How can you help us?

None of these requests are bad. In fact just the opposite. They show a proactive partner that wants to evangelize about your product and spread the good word.

Next steps:

Understand who the target audience is? New partners may be off track and targeting the wrong people you already know will have little interest or with whom you have had limited success.

Return on Investment: What do they anticipate the end result will be? How many people are they looking to speak to? How many leads do they expect to get? What percentage of those do they hope to convert and what will be the value of that?

What is the ASK: They have come to you looking for something? Is that art work, approval on the promotion or to say something publicly. Do they want investment? Depending on what they are asking for and when may depend on if you can support at all. If your budget funds have been allocated and the partner is looking last minute for funding you may have to say no to even the best of proposals. Or go back to your internal teams looking for additional funding. This is not the best. We want to show that the channel is an organized and efficient department that has thought in advance and planned. However, sudden last minute opportunities do come up. As a Channel Manager you cannot say yes to everything and it is worth carefully considering when you go and grovell for additional funding and when you say no.

Skin in the game: This is an American term that means you have a personal investment in something and therefore a vested interest in its success. Is the partner asking for you to do 100% of whatever it is they want or are they putting some of their own "skin" (money, people, resources) in?

> *Tip: One thing that often comes up from leaders who do not understand the channel is "well aren't they going to contribute. They have no skin in the game". On the face of it this may be true but go back to our section on return on investments and what's in it for them.*
>
> *By the time the partner gets to this stage they will have invested a considerable amount of time in things like your training, learning your technology, systems and an announcement. That is their skin in the game. Imagine your ROI for the partner has them making $500 after 3 months of work involving 3 people on their small team. Yes, it may be worthwhile in the end when it becomes a volume business and it only takes one member of their team, but right now they need your help.*
>
> *You can (and we do!) debate this with other departments frequently. The bottomline here is that a partner will limit how much they invest until they have started making money. Helping them here reduces the speed to market. Think of it as not giving money to a partner but rather a marketing expense that you would have had in some way if you tried to enter a new market on your own.*

While a retroactive approach may yield some results, your utopia for marketing through your channel partners is Proactive partner marketing. In an ideal world you have worked collaboratively with your indirect teams in advance and come up with a collaborative marketing strategy that includes but is not limited to:

- A partner marketing budget
- A list of KPIs directly tied to marketing efforts
- Branded content for partners (emails, different lengths of wording, images, template ads, posters etc)
- Suggested campaign rollout schedule
- Calendar of events and speaking engagements with partner opportunities
- Social media templates formatted for the different platforms

> *Tip: Take a look at Partner Strategy template 3 for an example of a partner marketing touch point map*

The more you enable partners to be self-sufficient by proactively providing them with partner marketing they can send out with minimal effort, the more they will and the faster you will start to see results.

Partner Announcement Template

Request PDF's of all templates at globalsaleschannel.com

PARTNER and COMPANY come together

Date

Locaction (E.G Bristol, U.K)

—

PARTNER today announced that it has joined the COMPANY Reseller Network to bring cutting edge technology to solve the artificial intelligence gap within the education sector.

PARTNER is a leading value added solutions provider of state of art and globally proven education and training solutions across the UKI and DACH regions.

"We are excited about this new relationship which will allow PARTNER to offer COMPANY's services to our school, colleges and universities".

"This move is in line with our strategic goal of becoming a complete service provider for the education sector".

"We are delighted to welcome the PARTNER to the COMPANY partner community.

Their geographical reach, dedication to customer satisfaction and professional excellence positions them to be knowledgeable and valuable advocates for our technology" says Andrea Brown, Channel Manager.

PARTNER is committed to enhancing value relationships with our Clients and Business Partners by providing unparalleled knowledge based world class solutions and services through innovative processes as well as best practices that make a lasting positive impact in our customer's businesses.

About PARTNER
Insert general information about the partner history and locations here. This information can typically be copied from their LinkedIn profile or website.

About COMPANY
Do the same for your company inserting general background information and locations here.

> *Tip: To complement any partner announcement we like to do and suggest partner videos posted across social media channels. Lots of examples of these are available by connecting with Andrea Brown on LinkedIn and searching through previous posts. Links are also available on globalsaleschannel.com*

To give leads or not?

This sort of fits under the umbrella of partner marketing and lead generation. There can be quite heated and mixed views on this subject.

Example: You are a company based in California.

You have a Reseller in the Kingdom of Saudi Arabia (KSA).

A lead comes in via your traditional marketing efforts and as part of your standard workflow gets passed to your direct sales team. It turns out the prospective customer is based in KSA.

The partner who knows the customer and has sold other things to them gets to hear about the opportunity and is confused and annoyed about why they are not able to manage the opportunity.

The direct AE struggles through doing their best but making assumptions about the local conditions, with limited knowledge of local competitors and alternatives.

Here lies the conundrum. Do you:

   a. Continue letting the direct team to work on it or
   b. Pass it to the local partner in KSA?

Reasons to keep it

- You may not have confidence in the partner especially if they are new
- You may have an annoyed Account Manager if this lead falls in their territory and they now feel as if they have lost it and been short changed.
- Lack of knowledge around a particular product or solution. Sometimes partners are prevented from selling everything on the menu and certain things are "direct only"

> *Tip: Watch out for "I would have made my number if you had not passed on so many of my leads to channel partners". Quite often the reason why a lead is not passed on comes down to something internal and political that may rock the boat and not because we do not agree it would be the best way to serve the customer. We get frustrated with this as will most channel managers. This scenario should have been flushed out as part of your channel strategy, but it often is not. We have seen channel programs three years in that did not discuss this and then hey presto it occurs in real time with a customer that is now being fought over internally. Not good.*

Trade Shows

- They will likely know more about the customer and have more relationships with them than you do
- They will understand the culture, local nuances and speak the language
- They are there, onsite and ready to go and meet the customer in person to do a demo
- They can offer ongoing local support and keep the relationship going with frequent in person check ins

Of course we are biased and believe the best way to do this if you do not have your own local teams is your channel partner. The crux of this comes back to the reason for this book in the first place. Are you an organization that has truly embraced the channel or are we just playing at it?

One of the arguments here is what are we paying channel partners for? Aren't we giving them a commission to bring us net new customers? Why would we hand them business on a plate that we can close ourselves.

This argument is flawed in that you simply have a higher propensity to close business that is in a local region if you do not have a direct sales team there or familiar with that region and you do have a local partner.

We would recommend passing leads on in this scenario and tracking the leads you give a partner versus those they bring in themselves. There are partner relationships that exist solely off the leads a vendor gives them. You do all the marketing and simply channel any local leads to them. There is nothing wrong with this but it is not our preference. We like to see partners working, driving their own opportunities and we find that approach a little, well, lazy.

Passing a partner who works hard to generate their own leads and bring you success, an occasional lead is a reward. You can even build this into your partner tiering program and have this as something earned for attaining defined targets.

Demo Kits

Just like giving partners leads there can be some controversy around this.

- Do you give a demo kit to partners?
- Shouldn't they buy their own?
- Should all partners get a demo kit or just some?

We think it is perfectly reasonable and justified for partners to get a demo kit upon successful completion of a partner training program. You do not want to give them a barrier to selling. You would not deny your own direct sales people tools they need to be successful and the same should be true of partners.

This should be a cost considered as part of your partner program P&L and overall strategy.

Trade Shows

Andrea wrote a tongue in cheek article years ago about why trade shows are a waste of time. Of course they are not but you have to use them properly rather than sit behind a desk looking bored expecting someone to beg you for a demo. We are not debating the validity of trade shows here but rather giving a bit of guidance about them as it relates specifically to channel partners.

What often comes up is:

Should you pay for a tradeshow that a partner wants

All the same arguments related to skin in the game as discussed at length earlier apply here.

Marketing Development Funds (MDF) is a budget that allows partners to access funding based on criteria that you come up with.

Example

2 Team Members trained and certified

Partnership announcement made

2 social media posts per week

1 sale per quarter/10 sales accepted leads

= Matching MDF funds up to $2,000

Matching here means that the company matches what the partner is willing to put in making it a shared expense.

You can also do exactly the same thing with a swag catalog and create hoops for partners to jump through in exchange for goodies.

> *Tip: As we mentioned earlier, be careful with this. If you put too many barriers in place partners just will not do it or it will considerably increase the time it takes to get a partner active.*

Partner Enablement

Partner enablement is all about education. It is a fancy word that means teaching partners about your product or solution and business processes so that we are empowering and enabling them with the skills they need to go off and sell on your behalf.

What this looks like can vary widely.

> *Tip: Partner enablement should not be painful. The days of partners spending weeks attending your course are gone. Training should be bite sized, entertaining, clear and valuable.*
> *Remember different people and therefore partners learn in different ways. Some will like to read while others will learn better from a video. Provide a wide range of options that reiterate key messages over a period of time. There are lots of training aps and PRMs with mobile functionality that mean partners can learn while on the go waiting for a client meeting.*

Training is not a one time exercise. There should be ongoing learning keeping your solution front of mind with the partner. There may also be newcomers to the partner business that need to be trained up.

Whether you use remote basic training or in person, consider limiting what the excited partner needs to get done in the beginning and then creating a training pathway that involves shadowing members of your team or presenting back to you and some of your executives in a role play.

Partner enablement is dynamic in that as you have a new or updated offer you need to consider what you might need from partner enablement.

If you are lucky your company will have an enablement team with a partner enablement specialist. However we spent most of our careers without that luxury, rolling our sleeves up and creating PDFs, Quizzes and training videos ourselves. Don't get intimidated by the term "partner enablement" or discouraged if you only have very limited resources. If you know what you need to train partners on you can normally find some friendly internal sales engineers or sales leaders to help you craft what your partner component might look like. Do not be afraid to be scrappy! Here something is definitely better than nothing.

Partner enablement can also be educating partners on how to sell. If for example partners have been used to selling software and you now need to try and effect a mental and cultural shift to software you may need a partner sales enablement program around that. This calculator shows us an example of that.It allows the partner to talk an end user through their scenario and then makes the partner look good by presenting the calculations at the end.

Touch Point Calculator

The Cost of a Manual Process

Here we are counting the manual steps Involved in the of something simple like a bus.ness card.

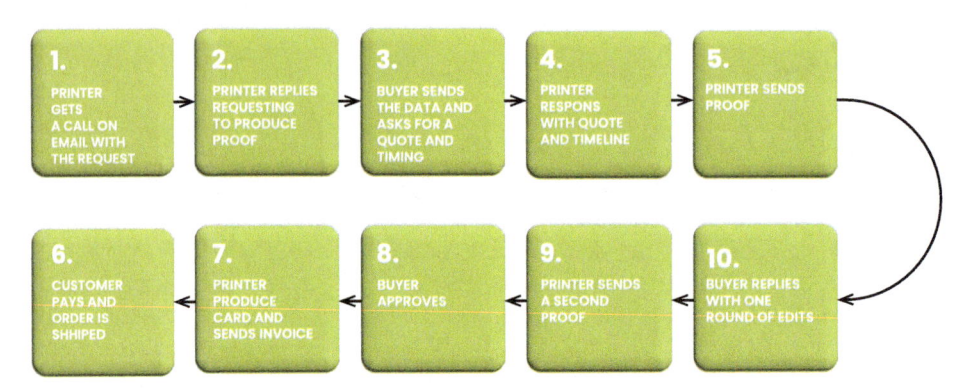

1. PRINTER GETS A CALL ON EMAIL WITH THE REQUEST	**2.** PRINTER REPLIES REQUESTING TO PRODUCE PROOF	**3.** BUYER SENDS THE DATA AND ASKS FOR A QUOTE AND TIMING	**4.** PRINTER RESPONS WITH QUOTE AND TIMELINE	**5.** PRINTER SENDS PROOF
6. CUSTOMER PAYS AND ORDER IS SHHIPED	**7.** PRINTER PRODUCE CARD AND SENDS INVOICE	**8.** BUYER APPROVES	**9.** PRINTER SENDS A SECOND PROOF	**10.** BUYER REPLIES WITH ONE ROUND OF EDITS

ecommerce replaces this process with an automated process= 1 step

You can count the steps of any process. In the example we have 10 touch points in the process.

So how long does each one take? The design may take an hour or a phone call may be 10 minutes. Agree on an average.

In this example it is 30 minutes.

Next, who does this work? Who takes the phone calls and responds to emails? Is It an admin assistant on a low wage or an owner of a small print shop who is hands on? Here an hourly rate of €7 per hour.

How of these business card orders does our printer produce in a month? In this exarnpfe the answer is 20.

You then multiply the numter of touch points by the average time it takes for one and the cost of the time associated with each one, to give you the manual cost per year for that one product.

Job Description Templates

Request PDF's of all templates at globalsaleschannel.com

Channel Manager

Role Description

This is a full-time remote role for a Channel Business Development Manager. The Channel Business Development Manager will be responsible for identifying and developing channel partners, creating business plans, managing accounts, and driving sales. The Channel Business Development Manager will also be responsible for creating and maintaining relationships with key clients and partners.

Skills Required

Business Planning and Channel Sales skills

Sales and Channel Partners skills

Account Management skills

Proven track record in business development and sales

Excellent communication and interpersonal skills

Ability to work independently and remotely

Experience in the technology or mobile device industry is a plus

Channel Operations

What You'll Be Doing...

- You will drive new partner acquisition, taking the lead personally where required
- You will be accountable for meeting our annual targets for new business
- You will be accountable for managing our portfolio of channel partners, identifying and pursuing opportunities to grow the Airwallex customer base and up-sell to existing accounts
- You will work with the EMEA Marketing team to define and execute against a Marketing strategy for channel partnerships, including relevant collateral and messaging
- You will communicate the company value proposition to channel partners and their clients, as well as more broadly within the ecosystem (e.g., at events)

- Traveling 50-75%

What You Bring...

- Experience of working with Digital Agencies, Development Agencies, and E-commerce Agencies
- Solid industry experience
- Experience working with data and spreadsheets
- 4+ years of work experience in a partnership role in a high-growth, scale-up environment (SaaS, FinTech or equivalent)

Who You Are...

- Results Driven - you hold yourself accountable for delivering on your targets
- Proactive - you identify, plan and execute against opportunities to grow
- Laser-Focused - you are ruthless in spending time on the highest-impact initiatives in a fast-paced environment
- Relationship Oriented - you can build deep and trusting relationships with partners
- Communicator - you have excellent written, verbal and in-person communication skills
- Leadership potential - you can step into the role of Lead across EMEA longer term

Director of Channel

The successful candidate will ideally be located in Brazil reporting to the MD Global Channels. As part of your day-to-day you will own the strategic direction of the channel, recruitment and development of partners aligned to the global channel partner program. You will be hands-on channel Business Director responsible for our success in the indirect business growth. Manage critical partner relationships, from identifying target partners, recruit, on-board, enable and provide in life management to accelerating business with existing partners. The role involves primarily commercial activities with dedicated channel technical support provided. The successful candidate will build a significant contribution to the regional business and help expand our partner ecosystem over time.

Key Interfaces: Sales Leadership, Pre-Sales, Sales team, Technical Account Management, Marketing, Vendors, Customers.

Responsibilities:

Be a hunter to recruit new partners aligned to the channel strategy

Farm existing partners to accelerate on boarding and drive increased activity

Support channel partner sales team in following sales methodology and best practices to help drive services portfolio.

Forecast channel business to the regional Sales leadership.

Develop metrics and outcomes to ensure global partner strategy is being executed and sales quota achievement whilst delivering feedback on performance at scheduled QBR's.

With the support of channel marketing lead, build and execute marketing plan and activities for the region leveraging channel coverage and relationships

Attend industry conferences and events to present and demonstrate the company's services offerings along with our partners

Business development activities to gain additional partner organizations involved and develop from prospective partners to successful revenue-generating partners

Lead our partner program execution in complex partner organizations/corporations through working with key stakeholders including marketing, product, innovation, and sales.

Enable and train commercially partner sales teams and channel technical teams with the support of the SE team, in order to drive success.

Enable new business value proposition through innovative commercial agreements with key selective partners.

Requirements:

10+ years of commercial experience, ideally selling security services, 5+ years of channel or partner experience.

Experience in selling Cyber Security services critically Managed Security – mandatory

Strong long term relationships and connections with partners across UKI - mandatory

Proven track record of recruiting and managing UK channel partners VARs MSP

Deep experience working with partners and ability to matrix manage and create win win strategies

Ability to build relationships across a wide range of styles and cultures to form networks within and outside the company

Adaptability, flexibility, positive energy and integrity

Excellent communication (written and verbal) and presentation skills

Willingness to travel

Becoming an invaluable partner

Much of this book has spoken to the channel manager, sales department or CEO wanting to expand their business internationally. The responsibility for making a channel partnership work is mutual. There can be lucrative rewards for being a successful channel partner and it may also be helpful for partners to understand the inner workings and expectations, particularly if they are new to partnering in this way.

Here are some guidelines for partners and how to become the very best invaluable partner you can be.

Remember this is a two way street. Just as a vendor is assessing you for the leads you can bring in, you should also be thoroughly assessing them.

Questions partners should ask during negotiations

- How established is the product or solution?
- How much success have they seen?
- Are they honest and transparent about bugs and development work?
- Is anything localized and what is their ability to do this? Does the product have technical limitations that may prevent this?
- What is the commercial pricing model? Does it account for multi currency and exchange rate variations? Is it aligned with what similar services are sold for in your region?
- If it is far more expensive do the benefits justify the cost and is this true in your local market?
- What launch tools and marketing templates are available to support you?
- Are there any additional costs for anything?
- Is funding available for launch events and marketing in order to establish the brand?
- What technical, sales and executive support is available to support you? How do you request it and how much notice is required?
- Does the company have a bid or tender department and is support from them available to partners?
- What is the process for training? How much time does it take and how many people on your team are required to complete it?
- What is the process to submit and track leads? How do they ensure that leads you submit are not contacted by the direct team or another partner without your approval?
- How do you get paid, what information is required from you and how long

does this take? If you are receiving a discount similarly understand what the internal approval process is for this and can you use your own purchase order or do they have a template.

> *Tip: As to speak with another partner who has been successful in a different market ideally outside of the home turf. They will not see you as a competitive threat and are usually willing to be transparent.*

Becoming invaluable

- Be active. Assign a specific person or team to manage this vendor. Ensure you set them KPIs around generating awareness, regular events, outreach and lead generation. This should support your partner agreement targets.
- Be visible on social media posting pictures, video and case studies about your actions and activities. Tag the vendor in.
- Be open to pilot programs and trying out new ideas. Offer to feedback to product development or be part of discussion forums.
- Show that you do have skin in the game. Calculate the personnel hours and any money invested keeping track of how this stacks up against returns.
- Take the extra time to generate good quality leads and provide detailed information if handing over to a direct sales team. Build a reputation of being efficient.
- Distributors need to be seen to be much more than order takers, which many have traditionally been, waiting until a reseller comes knocking based on an end user that has made a request to them. Today Distributors need to be much more proactive:
  - Ensure your team have been trained on and understand the solution
  - Don't expect the reseller to do lots of work to figure out why they should take something new and shiny to their clients. Provide the information the reseller needs.

Example:

Hey Jane

We have a terrific new vendor that I want to bring to your attention.

Should be a good fit for 90% of your finance clients

a) It integrates with their existing systems

b) It will allow them to speed up operations and increase profitability

c) It earns you 30% commission

Recent wins include: ABC Bank and XYZ Hedge Fund. Our team is fully trained on it.

Can we have a chat about outreach with a call to action around a demo as a next step?

- If something is not working well like the pricing model is not right for your market, document why and go armed with a suggestion coupled with how much more business you believe you would be able to achieve with those changes. Do not just miss your targets and complain.
- In instances where you have only been a buy through perhaps proactively be willing to reduce the commission/discount to acknowledge this.
- Ask new clients if they would mind providing some information for a case study. You could offer to write this with the vendor and then send it to them for approval. In new markets case studies are gold dust.
- Close business well. Do not over sell features and benefits just to win.
- Keep in touch regularly with clients, just to say hello or meet for a coffee and see how things are going. Bring them interesting ideas and suggestions that are not trying to sell them something. You want to identify anything they are not happy with so that you have the opportunity to fix it. Ultimately you want to be instrumental in the clients contract renewal or expansion.
- Network yourself throughout the vendor organization. Get to know other people other than your local channel manager and the channel team. Introduce yourself to the VP of sales, share your successes and ideas with them. Make sure you are on the radar.

Glossary

TERMS	MEANING
AE	Account Executive. Sometimes AM - Account Manager
ARR	"Annual Recurring Revenue" = the forward-looking annual revenue expectation of a subscription or group of subscriptions. Only products that are expected to be recurring are included. Hardware and product pilots, for example, are excluded from the recurring revenue calculation.
Burn	This refers to how much cash you are spending and how quickly you are spending it.
Carrot	Incentive
Caveats	Exceptions
Channel Exclusivity	Giving a channel partner exclusive rights to something, often a territory or a particular product.
Churn	Churn rate, sometimes known as attrition rate, is the rate at which customers stop doing business with a company over a given period of time. Churn may also apply to the number of subscribers who cancel or do not renew a subscription. The higher your churn rate, the more customers stop buying from your business.
COGS	Cost of Goods Sold = payroll and other expenses (such as cloud services) tied to the delivery and support of the product to the customer.
ConTech	Construction Technology
Core offering	The main or primary offer
CPA	Certified Public Accountant
CV	Contract Value
DACH	An abbreviation. DACH stands for D — Deutschland (Germany), A — Austria, CH — Confœderatio Helvetica (Switzerland). Therefore, it refers to German-speaking Europe.
Disti	Short for Distributor
Efficiency Score	Efficiency Score = change in ARR from prior period to the current period / Cash Burn (from operating and investing activities)
EMEAI	Europe, Middle East, Africa and India
Fiscal YE	Fiscal Year-End; refers to the completion of a one-year or 12-month accounting period rather than a typical calendar year eg our Fiscal YE date is Jan 31.
FY21	Fiscal Year '21

TERMS	MEANING
GDP	GDP measures the monetary value of final goods and services—that is, those that are bought by the final user—produced in a country in a given period of time (say a quarter or a year). It counts all of the output generated within the borders of a country.
Gross Margin (%)	Gross Margin % = Gross Profit / Revenue
Gross Profit ($)	Gross Profit = Revenue - COGS
GSI's	Global Systems Integrators
H1 / H2	Indicates the first half (H1) of the fiscal year (months 1-6) and the second half (H2) of the fiscal year (months 7-12).
Happy ears	The tendency to hear what you want to hear rather than the reality.
Headcount	Headcount = full-time employees that are active at the end of a period such as at the end of a month
Hyper growth	Very fast growing companies
LATAM	Latin America
Lighthouse examples	Leading examples of how an individual or business successfully used your product or service. Like a testimonial or case study. Lighthouse examples are the first of their kind in a market shining a light on a new product or service.
Magic Number	Magic Number = A financial goal that a business needs to reach a certain level of break even or profitability. You can define what the magic number means for your organization.
MDF funds	Market Development Funds - Given to indirect teams to aid the channel in sales and marketing efforts.
New Logo	New company name that you are now working with
OPEX	"Operating Expenses" = Research and Development (R and D) + Sales and Marketing (S and M) + General and Administrative (G and A)
Phased approach	Doing something in sections one at a time rather than all at once
Pitch Deck	A sales presentation. Deck refers to the slides.
PRM	Partner Relationship Manager - software platform to help you manage partners.
Productized	Taking what you have to sell and packaging it up in a way that is sellable to a particular market group or audience.
QBR	Quarterly Business Review
RASCI	Responsible, Accountable, Supporting, Consulted and Informed. It is a methodology for efficient team collaboration where what each person's role is on a project is defined into one of these categories.

TERMS	MEANING
Recky	The process of visiting and quickly looking around a place in order to find out information about it. This comes from the military term reconnaissance, a mission to find out about enemy, terrain, weather, positions, obstacles and routes.
Respondents	Those who participate in the survey.
Revenue	Income that is recognized in the same period that services are provided to the customer.
ROI	Return on Investment
ROW	Rest of World
SaaS	Software as a Service - licensing in which software is accessed online via a subscription.
SAOs	Sales Accepted Opportunities
SFDC	Sales Force dot Com - a CRM (customer relationship manager) software
SKU	Stock Keeping Unit
Track of work	Things to do
VARS	Value Added Resellers

About Andrea Brown

Andrea has worked with channel partners for over 20 years building and managing global channel strategies for organizations like GE, Xerox, AT&T, Nortel Networks and Procore Technologies. Andrea started her career "pounding the pavement" signing up anyone who would listen and has managed all different functions of the channel from operations to partner marketing. Andrea has been responsible for starting channel programs in EMEAI, APAC, North America and LATAM as well as managing global teams.

She has extensive relationships with Distributors, Resellers, Referral Partners, Global Systems Integrators and Integration partners. Many of whom she has worked with for 10+ years and now considers friends.

Voted a Top 40 executive under 40 by Crain's New York, privately she is deeply passionate about helping the homeless or those in extreme poverty and started charity soap4all.com in 2015.

Most importantly she is mum to two National level competitive swimmers Jack and India and is committed to improving mental health for youth athletes.

About Belinda Brown

Belinda Brown holds a Master's degree in Business. She is Director of Marketing and Business Development for Gazelle Global Research Services. The company focuses on qualitative and quantitative research now celebrating its 30th year under the leadership of Anne Brown serving some of the largest global brands from healthcare to retail and more.

Belinda sits on the Board of Directors for her chapter of the Insights Association and the Associate Board of Directors for the Marketing Research Education Foundation (MREF).

She considers giving back to her industry and her community more broadly to be of paramount importance.

Belinda is an activist and an advocate passionate about maternal/fetal health and social justice.

Special thanks

Many thanks to Veronica Le Cheminant for proofreading and editing.

We are extremely grateful to all our business partners that contributed recommendations. These views are their own and do not necessarily reflect endorsements from the companies they work for.

Request PDF's of all templates at globalsaleschannel.com

Printed in Great Britain
by Amazon